Twisting Arms

Teaching Students How to Write to Persuade

Dawn DiPrince

D1402110

Cottonwood Press, Inc
Fort Collins, Colorado

Requests for permission should be addressed to:

Cottonwood Press, Inc.
109-B Cameron Drive
Fort Collins, Colorado 80525

E-mail: cottonwood@cottonwoodpress.com
Web: www.cottonwoodpress.com
Phone: 1-800-864-4297
Fax: 970-204-0761

ISBN 978-1-877673-65-8

Cover design by Chris Gregori

Printed in the United States of America

Table of Contents

Using this Book

While teenage students often appear aloof and apathetic, that appearance is, for the most part, only a facade. Adolescents are anything but apathetic. They run hot and cold. They love things or hate them. They are for things or against them. Often, there are no in-betweens.

While teenagers are often inappropriately dogmatic, teaching them the art of persuasion can help them channel their hidden passions and absolute opinions more constructively. Don't get me wrong; I'm not saying that persuasive writing is a cure for adolescent angst. Persuasive writing can, however, give teenage students something positive to do with their overflowing opinions about the world.

Learning the art of persuasion has never been more important. Everywhere we turn in modern society, from political pundits to marketing schemes, we are bombarded with persuasive tactics. Today's students need to learn the art of persuasion both to use it themselves and to deal with it in their everyday lives.

Twisting Arms is full of easy-to-use activities that will sharpen writing and persuasion skills. It also includes helpful information on conducting research, avoiding plagiarism, rebutting arguments, and more. Best of all, *Twisting Arms* helps students start with a topic they are already passionate about and funnel their opinions into an organized and persuasive paper.

While this book covers a lot of information, it is designed so that teachers can pick and choose the activities best suited for their classrooms. Use the book as an integral part of a large persuasive writing unit, or choose various activities throughout the year to focus on different skills.

Even though the art of persuasion is thousands of years old, teaching persuasive writing can still be fresh and alive. I hope you find the activities, ideas and tools in *Twisting Arms* useful in your classroom. More important, I hope that your students enjoy and learn from the experience of becoming persuasive writers.

Dawn DiPrince

Writing to Persuade

An Introduction

The activities that follow are designed to serve as an introduction to persuasive writing. They provide background and allow students to learn about and practice some important principles of persuasive writing before they actually attempt to write a persuasive paper or essay themselves.

This section also includes information about many of the propaganda techniques that are commonly used for persuasive purposes.

What Is Persuasive Writing?

Persuasion takes many forms. It is everywhere in our daily lives, from commercials to billboards to cartoons to newspaper stories. Often, it is used in writing.

What is persuasive writing, exactly? It is any type of writing that attempts to persuade us to adopt a point of view, agree with an opinion, take an action, form a belief, etc. It is any type of writing that involves an *argument*.

For the next few days, pay attention to the forms of persuasion that surround us. Find three examples of arguments and bring them to class. Choose from the following:

- A letter to the editor
- An editorial
- A cartoon
- An advertisement
- A newspaper article
- A written description of a radio or television commercial
- A written description of an argument you heard in a discussion or a lecture
- Any other example of material that contains an argument

Follow-up

For each of the three examples you found, answer the following questions:

1. What is the *issue?*

2. What is the *argument* or *point* that the piece is trying to make?

3. Does the piece make effective arguments? Is it convincing?

4. What would you change to make the argument or arguments more effective?

Point of View

Every piece of writing, including persuasive writing, comes from a specific *point of view* or *perspective*. If you and your brother get into a fight, you are likely to give a very different account of events than he will. You will probably say that he started it. He will say that you did. You will both be telling the story of the fight from a different *point of view.*

Have you ever known a couple who broke up? If you talk to both people from the ended relationship, you will likely get two very different accounts of how and why they broke up. She might tell you they broke up because he was too boring, while he might say they broke up because he was interested in someone else. The two people will be telling the story of the break-up from two different perspectives.

All persuasive writing has a point of view. If it's your paper, it will be from your point of view, of course. If it's by someone else, it is important to look at that point of view. If a piece is telling how a political candidate is a brilliant, highly talented leader, it is important to know that it is being written from the point of view of the campaign manager. If a piece tells how the same candidate is an incompetent nincompoop, it is important to know that it is being written from the point of view of her opponent's campaign manager. Point of view has a definite impact on the content of any kind of writing.

Directions

Practice looking at how point of view influences a story. Imagine a fairy tale told from the point of view of each of the characters involved. Cinderella might first tell the story from her point of view, beginning something like this:

> *My dad used to have good taste in women. He married my beautiful, kind mother, didn't he? After she died, though, he settled for my stepmom, who is nothing but a mean, hateful old hag.*

The wicked stepmother might then tell the story from her point of view, beginning something like this:

> *When I first met my husband, I should have known he was too good to be true. If I had known then that I'd be saddled with this lazy, worthless stepdaughter, I would never have agreed to marry him.*

Now try telling the story of Little Red Riding Hood from the point of view of each of the main characters. (You may need to review the story first. Look it up in the library or on the Internet, if necessary.) Retell the story from the perspective of each of the following characters:

- Little Red Riding Hood
- The grandmother
- The wolf
- The woodcutter

The Dead Greeks

An argument can sometimes get a person into trouble—with parents, with teachers, with public officials, or even with friends. Still, the argument has a very sophisticated and ancient history.

Way before American malls boasted a gyro shop in the food court, Greece was well-known for something else—the birth of Western Civilization. Around 2,300 years ago, three men helped to change the way we live. The three men were Socrates, Plato, and Aristotle. Socrates, the oldest, taught Plato, and Plato taught Aristotle.

With long white beards to match their flowing togas, these Greeks developed and refined the art of persuasion. They believed that argument or debate was the highest form of discussion and that it could eventually reveal the highest ideals or truths. Men of ancient Greece would gather or walk around and literally argue for the sake of arguing. Those who could argue both sides of an issue, regardless of their own beliefs, were highly admired.

Socrates. Socrates was an inventor of sorts. Unlike Thomas Edison and Alexander Graham Bell, who invented tangible things, Socrates invented something intangible—the art of philosophical discussion. After inheriting money upon the death of his father, he devoted his life to engaging in discussion with young people from wealthy families in Athens. He questioned their confidence in the truth of popular opinion. Because of his insight into moral character and popular opinion of the time, Socrates had a very loyal following of young people. However, their parents became leery of his influence over their children. He was eventually charged with corrupting youth and meddling with religion. He was convicted and sentenced to death, but he beat the prosecutors to the job. Socrates killed himself by drinking hemlock while surrounded by friends and family.

Most of what is known about his ideas comes from the writings of Plato.

Plato. Plato was a student of Socrates. He also studied under Pythagoras, the mathematician famous for the Pythagorean Theorem ($a^2 + b^2 = c^2$). He established his own academy in Athens to pass along mathematical theories and the philosophical vision of Socrates. In his writings, Plato tackled questions of morality, such as "Can virtue be taught?" and "Is it ever justified to defy the rules of the state?" In his most famous work, *The Republic*, he wrote about the nature of justice and the virtues of wisdom, courage and moderation. Some of Plato's writings also examined different forms of government and the notion of a perfect society.

Aristotle. Aristotle spent 20 years of his life studying at Plato's Academy in Athens. After Plato's death, he became a teacher in his own right and later created his own school in the Lyceum in Athens. He spent his life examining a variety of topics, including logic, philosophy, ethics, physics, biology, psychology, politics and rhetoric. (Rhetoric is the art of using words effectively in speaking and writing—a useful skill in arguing a point.) His aim was to develop a universal method of reasoning that would make it possible to learn everything there is to know about reality.

While Socrates, Plato and Aristotle are long dead, their ideas still impact our lives today. Below are three important foundations of U.S. society that can trace their roots to the ideas discussed and debated by these ancient Greeks:

The First Amendment. Like the ancient Greeks, the founders of the United States believed in the importance of freedom of speech. They believed such freedom would allow a "marketplace of ideas," where any idea could be thrown out for discussion. The First Amendment to the Constitution protects our rights to freedom of speech, press, religion, assembly and petition.

Universities. Higher education began in 387 B.C. when Plato created his ancient Greek Academy. Students were taught to discuss and debate difficult questions, like "What is the meaning of life?" Eventually this discipline of debate and discussion became the center of a liberal arts education, which is the foundation of many of today's universities. Even today on university and college campuses across the country, you can find groups of students engaged in lively debate with their teachers.

Congress. Before a bill can become a law, it is debated and discussed in committee meetings or on the floor of the House of Representatives or the Senate. The result is that legislators can change minds or create compromises that ultimately ensure a bill's passage into law. Debate, argument, and persuasion grease the wheels of government.

Directions:

Here are some of the questions commonly debated by the Greeks. In small groups, choose one of the questions for discussion. Remember that the Greeks believed in questioning, questioning, questioning. As you discuss, ask people for clarification. Dig deeper. Imagine that there are no right or wrong answers.

- What is courage?
- What does it mean to be a good person?
- Is it ever justified to defy the rules?

Important Note: A Greek-style argument does not include loud yelling, name calling or getting angry. You must remember to be dignified and to steer clear of personal attacks.

Fact vs. Opinion

To write a persuasive paper, you must present an opinion. You've got to make a point and try to convince others that your opinion is the correct one.

You can't write a persuasive paper about, say, "penguins." You might write a *report* on penguins, or an informative paper. However, you would not be trying to persuade readers of anything. You would just be *telling* them about penguins.

Papers that just give information are filled with facts. Papers that persuade must be filled with facts *and* opinions.

What is a fact?

Christopher Columbus told everyone that the world was round, but no one believed him. At the time, everyone thought the world was flat. However, as the story goes, in 1492 Columbus sailed the ocean blue to prove his point. He demonstrated that the earth is round, and since then satellites have sent us actual photos of our round earth, giving us further proof. It is a *fact* that the earth is round.

A fact is a piece of information that can be confirmed or verified. For example, you can confirm that sea water tastes salty. (Simply have someone take a sip of it.) You can confirm that Johnny Depp was in *Pirates of the Caribbean*. (Go to a video store and check out a copy.) You can confirm that the sky looks blue to those on earth. (Just go outside and look up.)

What is an opinion?

An opinion, on the other hand, is simply a point of view that someone holds. It is a *fact* that some tomatoes are red. It is an *opinion* that tomatoes taste disgusting. It is a fact that *The Simpsons* is a television show. It is an *opinion* that it is the funniest cartoon on television.

It is important to know the difference between fact and opinion when writing or researching a persuasive paper. Test your ability to distinguish between fact and opinion. For each question below, mark either F (fact) or O (opinion).

___ 1. Zac Efron stars in *High School Musical.*

___ 2. Zac Efron is a hot babe.

___ 3. Born Harold Jenkins, country singer Conway Twitty took his stage name from Conway, Arkansas, and Twitty, Texas.

___ 4. Country music sounds like a group of dying alley cats.

___ 5. Fall is the best season because of milder temperatures and the changing leaves.

___ 6. Monster Truck-A-Thons are tacky.

(continued)

___ 7. SPAM online is even more annoying than phone calls from telemarketers.

___ 8. In the cartoon, SpongeBob SquarePants lives in a pineapple under the sea.

___ 9. *SpongeBob SquarePants* is the best cartoon on television.

___10. Katie Holmes looks way better with long hair.

___11. Katie Holmes is married to Tom Cruise.

___12. Dale Earnhardt earned over $27 million racing cars in his lifetime.

___13. Dale Earnhardt is the best race car driver who ever lived.

___14. Teenagers are more responsible than their parents think.

___15. The legal voting age should be lowered to age 16.

___16. Split pea soup should be banned from all school cafeteria menus.

___17. Ansel Adams used black and white film to take photographs.

___18. Colorado is the coolest state to live in because of its winter sports.

___19. The Statue of Liberty is a popular tourist destination.

___20. Tony Hawk is a professional skateboarder.

___21. Dubai has a large indoor ski area.

___22. A hybrid vehicle runs on a combination of gas and electricity.

___23. Leonardo DiCaprio is the best actor ever.

___24. Listening to classical music is lame.

___25. Gettysburg is the site of the largest battle of the Civil War.

___26. Wii is superior to PlayStation3.

Propaganda Techniques

Throughout history, propaganda has been used to help influence the way people think. Propaganda involves carefully using words or pictures in a certain way in order to influence opinions, emotions, attitudes and behavior. Propaganda is all around us, in commercials, in ads, in political campaigns, in company annual reports, in press releases, etc. It can be used for both positive and negative purposes.

It is important to be able to recognize common propaganda techniques. When you recognize them, you are better able to resist pressures to think or feel a certain way—except when you agree that thinking or feeling that way is a good idea.

Bandwagon involves the argument, "Everyone is doing it, so you should, too." In other words, you should "jump on the bandwagon" and think/do/act/look a certain way. The technique is very much like peer pressure.

Testimonial is used when an important person or famous figure endorses a product or an idea. The underlying message is that if this important person believes something is a good idea, it must be. Commercials often use this technique when they show a famous person using a product.

Transfer is the technique of using symbols that pack a strong punch with their message. The symbol might be something people either widely respect or widely despise. For example, the American flag can stir strong emotions. That's why political candidates try to stand in front of as many flags as possible. They are trying to "transfer" the good feelings people have about the American flag onto themselves.

Repetition is based on the idea, "If you repeat something over and over again, people will believe it." Sometimes political candidates accuse their opponents of having done something undesirable, and they repeat the charges in commercial after commercial. Whether or not the charges are true, people often start believing them, simply because they have heard them so often.

Plain Folk is a propaganda technique that uses ordinary people or "plain folk" to gain the confidence and trust of the audience. Plain folk fit most people's image of decent, everyday people. They speak in simple, straightforward language and use common sense. Plain folk advertising uses words such as "family," "children," "home" or "neighbors" to convey a warm, down-to-earth, home-like feeling.

(continued)

Directions:

Each of the following describes a commercial. What propaganda techniques are used in each?

1. A 35-year-old woman from the Midwest says, "I don't know much about newfangled technology, but I do know I like using World Online Internet service to e-mail my daughter who moved to New York City. It just brings her closer to home."

   _____

   _____

2. An ad shows the attacks on the World Trade Center, and then cuts to a red, white and blue background. This text is displayed: "Don't be caught off guard. Buy Commerce State Life Insurance. Don't leave your loved ones unprotected."

   _____

   _____

3. An ad shows a basketball player dunking the ball. He says, "Milk is great." A woman is shown running and catching a subway. She says, "Milk is great." A teenage boy is shown on a date with the cutest girl in school. He smiles and says, "Milk is great." A baby is shown happily playing. Her shirt says, "Milk is great." A beautiful model with a healthy glow says, "Milk is great."

   _____

   _____

4. An ad shows a group of cute young people walking and dancing in Times Square. They are all wearing the same style of flat-front khakis. Text comes up saying, "Join the Club. Wear Club Khakis."

   _____

   _____

5. A man is at home with his kids while his wife is on a trip. The kids have made a big mess in the kitchen. He says, "At times like this, I wish I knew more about keeping the house clean. But, thankfully, there is ForestSheen. It cleans everything...and, I mean *everything*. My family would be lost without it."

   _____

   _____

Follow Up:

Find one example on television or in print for each of the techniques listed on the previous page. Identify the propaganda technique(s) being used in each example.

War Propaganda

Teacher Instructions

"When you ride alone, you ride with Hitler!"

"We can do it!"

The statements above are well-known messages from American propaganda posters used by the U.S. government in World War II. They are, of course, examples of propaganda used for a good purpose—the defeat of Adolph Hitler. For a look at World War II propaganda posters, visit the exhibit on the National Archives web site. The posters can be found at this address:

www.archives.gov/exhibits/powers_of_persuasion/powers_of_persuasion_intro.html

The posters are interesting because they lack the finesse and subtlety of modern marketing. The messages are direct, harsh and blatant. For example, one poster asks civilians to sacrifice, using the image of a dying soldier and the words, "You talk of sacrifice. . . he *knew* of sacrifice."

The obvious propaganda techniques found on the World War II posters are a perfect way to jumpstart a discussion about persuasion. As a group, discuss and analyze the posters. Select a few posters of different types and have students answer these questions:

1. What is the poster's message? Is this message conveyed mainly with art or with words?

2. Who is the message for?

3. What colors are used on the poster? How do they help "shade" the message?

4. What symbols are included on the poster? Are they negative or positive symbols? Are they weak or powerful?

5. Is the poster successful in promoting its message? Why or why not?

New Propaganda

The concept of advertising really spread its wings in the 1950s, with the popularity of television. Growing numbers of Americans were suddenly exposed to lively, frequent commercials, right in their living rooms for the whole family to see. Because they had never before been exposed to propaganda techniques on a daily basis, people were generally more vulnerable to advertising ploys.

One result was that the marketing world helped create an image of a squeaky-clean, happy and wholesome America, with mothers wearing high heels and aprons as they happily cleaned the house. It was also a white world, with no images of blacks or other minorities. Advertising tended to create *one* image of society and to suggest that everyone should strive for that image.

Things are very different now. People today tend to be more cynical and jaded about advertising. They don't trust the media and say things like, "That's just a marketing scam." As a result, advertising has evolved to fit the times we live in. Marketing firms spend millions of dollars every year on databases full of information that targets customers' specific subcultures. Is someone a skateboarder? A yuppie? An environmentalist? A working mom? There are ads that target just about every kind of group imaginable.

People are so much shrewder about marketing today that advertising often goes underground. For example, "product placement" is huge now. Companies pay to have their products mentioned or shown on television shows or movies. Sometimes, they even pay to have whole story lines built around a product. Such tactics tend to be more believable because they don't yet "seem" like advertising to most people.

Some of the changes in advertising techniques are also technology-driven. Remote controls allow people to mute commercials. TIVO allows them to skip commercials altogether. Satellite radio allows them to avoid radio advertising. With the Internet, marketers find it easier to target specific groups, like alternative music fans, mystery book lovers, Yu-Gi-Oh card collectors, or just about any other subgroup or subculture.

While tried and true marketing techniques like "bandwagon" and "testimonial" are still used today, some of the following propaganda techniques are becoming more popular:

Otherness. The bandwagon technique of marketing says, "Everybody is doing it, and so should you." Otherness is just the opposite. It says, "*Not* everybody is doing this, but you are special, so you should." For example, an ad for a hybrid car might suggest the message, "Everybody drives a gas-guzzling SUV, but not you. You are special. You care about the environment, so you should drive our car." "Otherness" marketing promotes an elite mentality that makes consumers feel they are just one of just a few in a very exceptional club.

Mass Marketing to a Subculture. A subculture is a smaller group of people within the main culture—golfers, Nascar buffs, science fiction readers, retirees, etc. In the past, advertising focused on what was supposedly the average American. Now, more and more marketing targets various subcultures. For example, some shoe commercials are designed to appeal only to runners. Some truck advertisements try to attract men who see themselves as "macho."

Interestingly, mass marketing to a subculture can actually help make that subculture more mainstream. For example, the record industry used to largely ignore hip-hop music. However, when companies like Def Jam Records demonstrated that there was money to be made in marketing hip-hop, the music moved onto a wider stage. The mass marketing of hip-hop brought urban clothes, music and slang to more Americans, even in rural areas. This, in turn, meant more people wanted to buy hip-hop products.

Collective Memories.
Collective memories are memories shared by large numbers of people, because of a common experience. For example, the tragedy of 9/11 is a memory that most Americans, unfortunately, share.

Because shared memories can be so powerful, marketers' campaigns often refer to them in their ads. The intent is to stir our emotions and sometimes our fears. For example, an airline company might use collective memories of 9/11 in ads featuring the safety of its planes. The ads would reflect back on our shared fear of airplane hijacking.

Humanizing Technology.
Old advertising techniques used "scientific" mumbo jumbo to convince consumers that their products were cutting edge. For example, a commercial might say, "This shampoo rebuilds split ends with its lab-tested mamahaca polymers."

Today advertisers often try to humanize or simplify their products, especially if they are technological in nature. Instead of using technological or scientific terminology, they will say things like, "This computer program is the friendliest one on the market," or "Taking pictures with this camera is a snap. You just point and shoot." Humanizing technology is effective partly because it appeals to people's needs and desires. It also works because consumers have grown suspicious of advertising that uses words that they don't understand.

Strong Women.
Advertising has always used beautiful women to sell everything from lipstick to Jell-O to motorcycles. In the past, ads usually portrayed women as gentle and weak and in need of help. Today, however, images of beautiful women are often strong and more athletic, representing both beauty *and* power. The athletic image of a woman in advertising today often suggests, "With this product, I am beautiful, strong, determined, and in charge of my life."

Directions

Create five mini-posters that showcase "new" propaganda. Find newspaper or magazine ads that use each of the following propaganda techniques:

- Otherness
- Mass Marketing to a Subculture
- Collective Memories
- Humanizing Technology
- Strong Women

Cut out the ads and mount them on construction paper or poster board. Above each ad, note the propaganda technique(s) being used.

Art and Persuasion

Diego Rivera. Michael Moore. Maya Angelou. Bob Marley. Trey Parker. What do these five people have in common? They have used protest art—murals, film, poetry, reggae music and cartoons—as a form of persuasion. "Protest" art refers to art that is used in a persuasive way to protest, challenge, or even make fun of certain ideas.

In 1933, for example, Nelson Rockefeller, one of the richest men of the time, commissioned Mexican artist Diego Rivera to create a mural at Rockefeller Center in New York City. The mural was to depict "Man at the Crossroads Looking with Hope and High Vision to the Choosing of a New and Better Future." Rivera protested capitalism by creating a mural with pro-Communist and anti-capitalist images. Rivera said, "I was quite aware that I was going against public opinion." Rockefeller eventually removed Rivera from the mural project and in 1934 ordered that the mural be destroyed.

Protest art can be a very effective form of persuasion. It uses a paintbrush, poetry, film or other mediums to create images that tweak our emotions. While persuasive writing uses mostly logic and words to persuade, persuasive art relies on the creation of images. Images can be created in many ways. Film, paintings, cartoons, etc., rely on images you can *see*. Poetry and songs use words to create images that you can *imagine*.

Directions

Look up the following examples of protest art.

1. Pablo Picasso's "Guernica"
2. "I, Too, Sing America," by Langston Hughes
3. "Blowin' in the Wind," by Bob Dylan
4. Cartoons from "Dr. Suess Goes to War"
5. "Still I Rise," by Maya Angelou

For each piece of art, write a paragraph that answers these questions. Do not read what the "experts" have to say about the art. Explain what *you* see.

- What images are used?
- What message do the images send?
- What were they protesting? Challenging? Making fun of?

The Basics

Learning About Arguments

A persuasive paper basically does two things: (1) It makes a point and (2) It supports that point with evidence. To say it another way, the paper expresses an opinion and then gives reasons why that opinion is correct.

    This section gives students practice in making a point and defending it, before they actually try to write a persuasive paper.

Declaring Yourself

Y ou have learned about the Declaration of Independence, written by Thomas Jefferson. However, have you ever really thought about what it *is*? It is exactly what the title says it is— a declaration.

The Declaration of Independence boldly declares that the United States of America has become an independent country. Brand new countries often use a declaration both to chart their paths and to be taken seriously.

A persuasive paper does the same thing. It makes a declaration. (The declaration eventually becomes part of the *thesis statement*, but more on that later.)

Declarations are easy to write. They come from your gut. They are not meant to be elegant. Writing a declaration is simply a way to begin molding your argument.

Practice

Make a declaration for each of the topics below. Think of gladiators or knights as they engage in battles. Wield your pencil like a sword and make each declaration strong and powerful. Here are two examples:

Topic: *Peanut butter and jelly sandwiches*
Declaration: Peanut butter and jelly sandwiches are the perfect food.

Topic: *Water quality*
Declaration: Every American has the right to a clean, uncontaminated glass of water.

1. **Topic:** *The environment*
   Declaration:

2. **Topic:** *Music sharing on the Internet*
   Declaration:

(continued)

3. **Topic:** *Going on a diet*
   Declaration:

4. **Topic:** *Censorship*
   Declaration:

5. **Topic:** *Country music*
   Declaration:

Active Persuasion

Teacher Instructions

The purpose of this exercise is to give students practice writing statements that make a declaration or express an opinion. Have students get into groups of three to five each. Explain that you will announce a topic, and students will then have 5-10 minutes to brainstorm as many different declarations as possible for that subject. Point out that students do *not* need to agree with the statements they write. What is necessary is that the statements express a clear opinion. For example, if the subject is "cell phones," students might come up with some of the following declarations:

- Cell phone use should be permitted in class.
- Driving while talking on a cell phone should be illegal.
- Cell phone etiquette should be taught in elementary school.
- Cell phone users are some of the most inconsiderate people around.
- In today's world, it is rude *not* to have a cell phone.

If the subject is "college," students might come up with statements like these:

- Every boy or girl should have a chance to go to college.
- College should be free for any student with decent grades.
- A college degree is a waste of time if you want to work as a computer programmer.
- No serious college student should ever join a sorority or a fraternity.
- Out-of-state college tuition rates should not be more expensive than in-state rates.

After the first five-minute brainstorming session, have students share their answers. If some of the statements don't really express an opinion, try having the class agree or disagree with those statements. (Example: *Cell phones now come with everything from text messaging features to cameras.* It is impossible for students to agree or disagree with that statement because it doesn't express an opinion. It is simply a fact. Students will quickly catch on.)

Some ideas for topics follow. Choose topics that are appropriate for the age level and maturity of your students, of course.

- curfews
- *American Idol*
- teen pregnancy
- classical music
- video games
- YouTube
- explicit lyrics in rap music
- pets
- the movie rating system
- peas
- comic books
- Facebook
- taking photos with cell phones
- blogs

(continued)

Follow-up

After students have practiced writing declarations that express an opinion, have them practice giving reasons for an opinion. Choose a statement one of the students has written in the previous part of this exercise. Then have each group come up with three *reasons why* the statement is true. Explain that the students' personal opinions do not matter at this point. The point is to work on giving reasons why, whether or not they agree with those reasons.

After students have shared reasons why a statement is true, have them come up with *reasons why* the same statement is false. It may take some effort for students to let go of their personal feelings about a matter, but doing so is an excellent exercise in seeing the other side of an argument. Students need to be able to see the other side of an argument so that they can acknowledge valid points by the opposition and also so that they can refute points that aren't valid.

Because I Said So . . .

Most young people have had conversations like the following:

BOY: Why do I have to make my bed if I'm just going to sleep in it again?
MOM: Because I said so.

GIRL: Why do I have to come home at 10:00 p.m. when everybody else gets to stay out until midnight?
DAD: Because I said so.

"Because I said so" may be effective for parents. However, nobody, including parents, can use "because I said so" as reasoning in a persuasive paper. A persuasive paper must include the *reasons why* behind an argument. The reasons must be specific.

Here's an example of what *not* to write:

Everyone should watch *Lost* because I think it is so great.

This sentence, in essence, says, "Watch *Lost* because I said so."

Here is a much better argument:

Lost is the greatest show because it mixes flashbacks with flashforwards, Matthew Fox is a great smoldering actor, and it has some of the best scenes in television history.

Instead of relying on "because I said so," this argument gives three reasons why. Persuasive papers generally include *at least three reasons* that support the argument.

(continued)

Practice

For each of the arguments that follows, come up with three *reasons why*. (Play along even if you don't agree with the listed argument. Later on, you will have plenty of time to write about your own opinions.)

Argument: It's hard being the oldest brother or sister in a family.

    1. It is hard because . . .

    2. It is hard because . . .

    3. It is hard because . . .

Argument: The state should lower the driving age to 14.

    1. It should lower it because . . .

    2. It should lower it because . . .

    3. It should lower it because . . .

Argument: Being a vegetarian is not a wise choice for teenagers.

    1. It is not a wise choice because . . .

    2. It is not a wise choice because . . .

    3. It is not a wise choice because . . .

Argument: P.E. class is an important part of school.

    1. It is important because . . .

    2. It is important because . . .

    3. It is important because . . .

Follow-up

Come up with three arguments of your own. Then write three *reasons why* for each of the arguments. You might choose from some of these topics:

popular music	the environment	joining the military
war	chat forums	"Goth" culture
rules at school	Japanese animation	teenage drinking
texting	violent video games	wearing animal fur
cyber-bullying	movie ratings	SimCity
teenagers and credit cards	guns at school	curfews

Defending *the* Ridiculous

Teacher Instructions

Practice in supporting a point does not have to be an oh-so-serious exercise. In fact, some of the best practice can come from doing just the opposite—having students try to support *ridiculous* arguments. They can have some fun, stretch their brains, and gain some valuable practice giving *reasons why.*

Have students work in small groups. Ask each group to choose any three of the following arguments and then list at least three reasons of support for each.

- Chimpanzees should have the right to attend public school.

- All school drinking fountains should be filled with Gatorade.

- It should be illegal to chew your fingernails and toenails.

- Students should always be allowed 10 minutes at the end of every class to socialize.

- Students should be allowed to dress like Christina Aguilera at school.

- It should be illegal to wear pants that are too low-waisted.

- Everyone should be required to have at least one pet.

- The "Barney" song should be our new national anthem.

- Text messaging truly makes the world a better place.

- It should be illegal to use classical music as a ring on your cell phone.

- Reese's Peanut Butter Cups should be considered one of the basic food groups.

- You should not be allowed to use slang if you are over the age of 35.

- Belly-button piercing should be done when someone is an infant.

- No teenage drivers should be forced to drive any kind of minivan with wood grain panels on the sides.

- Police should take away the driver's license of anyone who repeatedly drives way below the speed limit.

- Kanye West should be elected President of the United States.

Practice Developing a Thesis Statement

Teacher Instructions

The activity that follows gives students practice in developing thesis statements. It can be handled in several ways. If at all possible, have students work in small groups, so that they can share ideas. Give the groups only *one* of the "Question Lists" that follow. The lists are arranged, very roughly, according to age appropriateness. In other words, the questions in "Question List #1" are generally ones that even younger students might have an opinion on. "Question List #2" includes a mixture of questions for different age levels. "Question List #3," the last list, includes items that are more appropriate for older students.

Each list includes a large number of questions. Students are to choose only three questions and develop a thesis statement around each.

Although they are to select only three questions, just reading over a list of questions can be very helpful to students. The list can give them ideas for avenues they might pursue when they write persuasive papers of their own.

Practice Developing a Thesis Statement

Every persuasive paper you write must include a thesis statement. A thesis statement answers the question, "What is your point?" It combines a declaration on your topic with the *reasons why* you believe the declaration is true. It serves as a road map to your paper, stating briefly—in only one sentence—what your opinion is, and why.

Your thesis statement should be written before you write your actual paper because it will help mold and guide what you write. As you write your paper, you may find you need to tweak your sentence to sound better or to better reflect the facts you discover in your research.

Practice writing thesis statements by following the directions below:

Directions

Select three of the questions from the "Question List" your teacher will give you. For each question, begin by writing a declaration—a bold opinion on the topic. Next, write at least three *reasons why* you believe as you do.

Once you have your declaration and your reasons why, mold all of that into one sentence, which will be your thesis statement. This isn't difficult, but it can take a little time. Here is an example:

Question: Should the FBI or police be able to see what books you have checked out from the library?

Declaration: It should be illegal for the government to see what books a person checks out from the library.

Reasons Why:
It is a violation of the First Amendment.
It violates our right to privacy.
It turns librarians into law enforcement officials.

Thesis statement: It should be illegal for the government to access someone's library records because to do so violates the First Amendment, violates our right to privacy and turns librarians into law enforcement officials.

Question List #1

1. Is it right for the government to require kids to attend school?

2. Should smoking cigarettes be illegal?

3. Would it ever be okay to arrest someone before he or she commits a crime?

4. Is our society too lenient with cheaters?

5. Do you deserve an allowance? Or a raise in your allowance?

6. Is homework necessary in order for students to learn?

7. Should students be able to attend school over the Internet?

8. Who should pay when a guy and a girl go on a date?

9. Are video games too violent?

10. Is it fair for teachers to give you a lower grade if you turn in an assignment late?

11. Should skateboarding be allowed on school grounds, parks, and public sidewalks?

12. Should unchaperoned young people be allowed into R-Rated movies?

13. Should young people be allowed to have a TV in their own room? Their own computer with Internet access?

14. Do rodeos promote cruelty to animals?

15. Is it fair for schools to require decent grades from students who participate in sports, student council, band, etc.?

16. Should you spay/neuter your pets?

17. Are schools for only one gender a good idea, i.e., schools for boys or schools for girls?

18. Should the legal age for driving be raised?

19. Should public school students be required to wear uniforms?

20. Should the legal age for drinking be lowered?

21. Is it okay for a public library to remove from its shelves books that people find objectionable?

22. Is it a good idea for schools to ban junk food and soft drink vending machines on school property?

23. Should middle school and junior high students be allowed to leave campus during the day?

24. Should parents refuse to let their children hang out with friends they don't like?

25. Should parents limit the time their children spend playing video games?

Question List #2

1. Are small schools better than large schools?

2. Should the law require people to wear seat belts?

3. Should prayer be allowed in public schools?

4. Is rock music better today than it was in the 1980s? 1970s? 1960s?

5. Should young people be allowed to buy cigarettes?

6. Will a woman ever become president?

7. Does prison reform people?

8. Does some rap music demean women?

9. Is it okay for men and women to use cosmetic surgery to remain youthful looking?

10. Is it okay for young people, like yourself, to have cosmetic surgery?

11. Should newspaper reporters ever have to reveal a confidential source?

12. Should teachers be paid more than professional athletes?

13. Should employers have the right to see your medical records?

14. Should there be a salary cap in professional sports?

15. Is the use of performance enhancing drugs casting a negative shadow on sports?

16. Is it wrong to eat animal products, such as milk and eggs?

17. Should pharmaceutical companies be allowed to advertise on television?

18. Do Americans spend too much time watching television?

19. Do Americans have a weight problem?

20. Are some people just born "bad"?

21. Can our founding fathers still be considered good men if they owned slaves?

22. Should a mother stay home with her young children, rather than work outside the home?

23. Should the Constitution be changed to allow people born in other countries to run for President of the United States?

24. Should foul language be banned on television?

25. Is "grounding" an effective punishment for young people?

Question List #3

1. Is the death penalty ethical?

2. Are taxes necessary?

3. Is capitalism the best type of economy?

4. Should a state recognize same-sex marriage?

5. Should the government help fund stem cell research?

6. Should the United States provide financial aid to foreign countries in need?

7. Should pharmaceutical companies provide low-cost or free drugs for AIDS victims in Africa?

8. Should the United States ever forgive foreign debt?

9. Should schools provide day care to assist teenage mothers?

10. Should drug addicts be sent to prison?

11. Should students be required to learn a foreign language?

12. Is it fair for school officials to be allowed to search student lockers and backpacks for drugs or weapons?

13. Is it fair that auto insurance rates are more expensive for males under the age of 21 than for females?

14. Is it ethical to do scientific research on animals?

15. Should schools teach creationism along with the theory of evolution?

16. Should the government fund artists through the National Endowment for the Arts?

17. Should major league baseball test its players for possible drug use?

18. Should people be allowed to gamble online?

19. Should the government tax purchases made over the Internet?

20. Should teenage murderers ever be sentenced to death?

21. Are people born innately good or evil?

22. Should the descendants of slaves be given reparations from the government?

23. Should health insurance pay for alternative health treatments, like massage, acupuncture or homeopathy?

24. Should the Federal Drug Administration (FDA) approve drugs for the marketplace more quickly?

25. Should states require citizens to obtain a license before becoming parents?

The Groundwork

Writing Your Own Persuasive Paper

This section takes students through the initial prewriting steps in the process of writing a persuasive paper of their own.

The Groundwork

When writing a persuasive paper, a lot of work needs to be done before you actually begin writing. Before you pick up a pencil or sit at a computer to write, you need to mull over ideas, think them through, and examine them from different angles. Professional writers do their "mulling" in a variety of ways. Some may think things over while they load the dishwasher or take a walk. Others may brainstorm, outline, or "web" their thoughts on paper before they actually start the writing process. J.K. Rowling, for example, filled notebooks full of outlines and ideas before she wrote the first sentence in her Harry Potter series. This process of thinking, mulling, outlining, and jotting things down is called prewriting.

The activities that follow are prewriting activities. They get your mind moving in the right direction and prepare you to write your paper. While all of these prewriting steps may seem time-consuming at first, they will usually *save* you time because they give your writing focus right from the start.

Prewriting steps for a persuasive paper:

1. Choose a topic.
2. Make a declaration.
3. "Web" or brainstorm for ideas.
4. Make a point.
5. Create a skeleton.

These steps are discussed in detail on the following pages.

Hot List

Before you ever begin to write a paper, it is smart to have a "Hot List." A Hot List, created throughout the school year, includes topics that you are interested in or want to learn more about. Keep the list in the back of your writing notebook, English folder or journal. Whenever you think of an interesting topic, add it to your list. When your teacher assigns a paper, it is easy to look over your Hot List for ideas.

Choosing a Topic

Choosing a topic is one of the most important steps in writing your paper. A topic can make or break your paper. If your topic is too big, it can be difficult to write about it without writing an entire book. If your topic is too narrow, you may be able to write only a single paragraph about it. The most important test, however, is if you are actually interested in your topic. Remember, it is going to take some time to write a persuasive paper. You will be living with your topic for a while, so you had better like it.

1. To choose a topic, begin by writing down some broad topic ideas you are interested in.
   Examples: cats, SPAM, TV, texting

2. Now narrow your topic to something more specific that you might write about.
   Examples: cat overpopulation, SPAM laws, TV decency standards, texting in schools

3. Finally, come up with a declaration about your topic.
   Examples:
   • All cats should be spayed or neutered.
   • Laws that prevent SPAM seem like a good idea, but they violate the First Amendment and will be hard to enforce.
   • The FCC has gone overboard trying to enforce decency standards and is violating the First Amendment.
   • Schools should allow students to text in school.

4. Finally, give your declaration the "Topic Test," on the next page.

(continued)

Topic Test

1. Am I interested in this topic?

2. Is this topic based on my opinion? (Remember, a persuasive paper must present an opinion. Otherwise it is just a report.)

3. Do I believe strongly in the opinion I will be writing about? (It can be difficult to write an entire persuasive paper if you feel ho-hum about your argument.)

4. Do I want to learn more about this topic? (You must do research on this topic to provide evidence to support your argument. If you think you already know everything about the topic and don't want to learn more, it will make doing research difficult.)

5. Is this topic too broad? (If there are entire books written on your topic, it is probably too broad. Narrow your topic further. For example, instead of writing about America's entire foreign policy, you might narrow the topic to your opinion of America's recent foreign policy in Somalia.)

6. Is this topic too narrow? (You must make sure that you can write a full paper on this topic. If your teacher has assigned a ten-page paper, and you think you can write only a couple of paragraphs on the topic, your topic is too narrow.)

7. Will you be able to find enough material? (You must be able to find supporting evidence in a variety of places. Be sure you can come up with at least three places, off the top of your head, where you are likely to be able to find information on your topic.)

Webbing

Think about a spider and her web. Starting in the center, she spins out branches from this main point. Then she continues to spin new lines from these branches.

You can do the same thing when thinking through your argument for a persuasive paper. Start by writing your declaration in the middle of a page. Focus on your declaration and spin off ideas from it. Take these ideas and spin more thoughts off of them. Continue until you have filled the entire page.

Example:

NOTE: Webbing is a way to brainstorm. When webbing, it is important to follow brainstorming rules:

1. Remember that when brainstorming, nothing is a bad idea. Put down everything you think of, without judging it. The more ideas you brainstorm, the easier it will be to write. (You can also choose to ignore any bad ideas later.)

2. Move quickly. You are not creating a work of art. Don't erase. Don't write in your perfect handwriting with little hearts over the *i*'s. Brainstorming is messy work.

Writing a Thesis Statement

Have you ever had a friend tell you a really long, really boring story? You can't concentrate on what he is saying because all you can think to yourself is, "What is his point? Does he even *have* a point?"

Your long-winded friend could benefit from a thesis statement. A thesis statement is one of the tools you use to keep your persuasive paper on focus. It is *one* sentence that answers the question, "What is your point?" It lets readers know what you are going to talk about in your paper and where you stand on the issue.

When you actually begin researching and writing your paper, you may refine your thesis statement. You are free to tweak the words, or even to change certain points after you have done more in-depth research. However, you should at least have a working thesis statement before you begin writing.

Follow the steps below to create a working thesis statement.

1. Write your declaration here.

2. What are the *reasons why* you believe as you do? Write at least three reasons here, if not more. Look at your webbing page to help you out.

3. Create your thesis statement, molding your declaration and your *reasons why* into one clear statement.

The Skeleton

Skeletons are not only a part of haunted houses and anatomy projects. They can also be an important part of writing. Before you begin writing the body of your persuasive paper, you should first build the skeleton.

A skeleton shows the bare bones of your paper. Once you have a skeleton, you can easily add the meat to your paper and flesh out your arguments. (Some skeletons are called "outlines" by English teachers. The kind of skeleton we are talking about here is a very basic one.)

Using a separate sheet of paper, follow the steps below to create a skeleton for your own paper. (Note: It is important to remember that your skeleton may change as you find out more information through your research.)

Step One. First, write your thesis statement. It is likely to become the powerful last sentence of your introduction.

Example:

A nutritious snack program would be a great addition to our district because it would allow schools to raise money, keep students from being hungry during the school day, help fight obesity in young people, improve student performance and teach students about nutrition.

Step Two. After your thesis statement, write out each of the *reasons why* that you have included in your thesis statement, leaving room to write after each one. Then add "gut information" to each reason why. Gut information is anything that you know or think you know, without doing research. Write things even if you are not 100% sure about them. You will be doing research, so you can delete anything that is false. Make notes about the items you definitely want to check on.

Example:

A nutritious snack program would still allow schools to raise money.

For some reason, schools always need to raise money.

Schools have used vending machines in the school to raise money in the past.

Some schools even have contracts with soft drink companies like Coca-Cola. (Research)

A nutritious snack program would keep students from getting hungry during the school day.

When students are hungry, they don't do as well in school.

Most students are still growing and generally need to eat during the day. (Research)

Hunger is distracting and can cause headaches and drowsiness.

A nutritious snack program would fight the growing obesity problem in young people.

The news keeps reporting that young people are fatter than they used to be. (Research)

We eat more junk food than we used to, which probably makes kids fatter. (Research)

Junk food is readily available at school, but healthy food isn't.

(continued)

A nutritious snack program would improve student performance.

Sugary snacks can also hurt student performance.

People eat junk food and get a sugar high but crash after 30 minutes. (Research)

A nutritious snack program would teach students about nutrition.

Schools are supposed to teach kids.

Offering junk food snacks just teaches kids that junk food is okay. (Research)

Offering nutritious snacks would teach kids how to make nutritious choices.

Step Three. For each of the reasons why, write down several questions that you have. Also write down where you might find that information.

Example:

A nutritious snack program would still allow schools to raise money.

For some reason, schools always need to raise money.

Schools have used vending machines in the school to raise money in the past.

Some schools even have contracts with soft drink companies like Coca-Cola. (Research)

Questions:

What is my school's policy on junk food vending machines? (Ask Principal DeLuca.)

Why do schools need to raise money? Where does it go? (Ask Principal DeLuca and look online.)

How many vending machines does my school have? (Talk to the janitor.)

How much money do our school vending machines make? (Ask Mrs. Leider in the office.)

What does it mean for a school to have a contract with Coca-Cola? Is it a school contract or a district contract? (Ask Principal DeLuca.)

When you have completed the three steps above, you will have a skeleton for the body of your paper. You also will have outlined the next steps you need to take before you begin writing.

Doing the Research

Collecting Information for Your Persuasive Paper

To be convincing in a persuasive paper, you must support your main point or thesis with evidence. Finding reliable evidence generally involves research of some kind. For those writing research papers, this section provides some very basic information about organizing research, taking notes, and citing sources. For complete information, it is important to consult a more detailed source, like the *MLA Handbook for Writers of Research Papers* or Purdue's Online Writing Lab (OWL): http://owl.english.purdue.edu/.

Of course, not every persuasive paper involves extensive research. Still, writers of any kind of paper may find parts of this section helpful.

Finding Evidence

*E*vidence! Evidence! Evidence! These are the first three rules of persuasion. You must provide evidence to support your thesis statement, or main point.

What if you were on trial for theft and the only thing your lawyer said to the court was, "This fine young person is not guilty because I like him, and I just know that he didn't do it." You would probably be looking at a conviction. Why? Your lawyer would have presented no evidence to support the claim that you did not steal. In other words, he would not have been at all persuasive.

To be persuasive, you need evidence. To have evidence, you need to do some research. While you may know a lot about a certain subject, you will need to back up what you know by looking up studies, talking to experts (or at least researching what they have to say), finding relevant statistics, etc.

The best way to begin research is by asking questions. If you have completed "Building a Skeleton," you already have questions. If not, take time to jot down some. What would you like to find out?

When you have written your questions, the next step is to think about where you can find the answers to those questions. Here is a list of possible sources:

- **Interviews.** For step-by-step instructions, see pages 52-54.

- **Reliable web sites.** It is important to stick with web sites from reliable sources. That involves using some judgment. For example, if you want to know the number of boxes of Cap'n Crunch cereal sold in 2002, you might go to the Quaker Oats web site for statistics. Since Quaker Oats sells the product, it would likely be a reliable web site for this information. It would not be smart to go to a teenager's web site for her list of "My All-Time Favorite Cereals."

  Use common sense. A web site with photos of someone's kittens or a list of the world's cutest boys is probably NOT a reliable web site.

- **Current magazines or journals** (nothing over 5 years old)

- **Current books** (nothing over 10 years old)

A computer with an Internet connection is, of course, a great tool for conducting research, as long as you are careful to choose reliable sites. Your school or public library is an invaluable resource for finding information in magazines and books. However, don't overlook other sources of information—namely, people. An interview can provide you with interesting and up-to-the-minute information.

Researching and Organizing

When doing research for a paper, it is very important that you find evidence from at least three different sources to support your main argument or thesis statement. If you find information from only one book, for example, your paper becomes more of a book report than a persuasive paper. The more research you do, the more reliable your information will be.

You will need to keep track of every source you use so that you can give credit for information taken from those sources. For a full-length research paper, your teacher will require a "works cited" page at the end of your paper. (If your class is not following the *MLA Handbook for Writers of Research Papers*, you may be asked to create a "bibliography" or "reference page" instead.)

Gathering research can take a lot of time and effort, so it is smart to make sure that your research results are organized in a way that is clear and easy to use. Here are some ideas for keeping track of the information you find during your research.

Compiling Research

Note Cards

Using note cards is the traditional way to keep track of research information. Note cards are simply 3" x 5" index cards.

With note cards, you put one item of information on each card—perhaps a quotation, a summary, a paraphrase, or a fact. You also write down information about *exactly* where you found that particular piece of information (author, title, publication date, etc.)

Of course, you don't want to have to write the same source information over and over again. That's why you create a "works cited" note card for each source you use. You write down all the information about a source *once* and give that source a code, like a number or a highlighter color. Then, every time you take a note from that source, you use that highlighter color or code number along with the page number where you found that information.

For example, suppose you give an article called "Hemingway's Big Fish" the source code #6. For every note you take from that article, you simply write #6, and then the page number of the information you are noting.

Advantages and Disadvantages of Note Cards. The note card approach works best when using more traditional sources, such as books, magazines, or journals. The best part about using note cards is that you can move them around. When organizing your paper, you can spread all of your note cards on the floor, table or even your bed. You can create a pile for each paragraph in your paper. If you are really a hands-on person, this may be the best approach for you.

A disadvantage of note cards is that it is easy to lose a single index card at the bottom of your backpack or the back of your locker.

Three-Ring Binders

Using a three-ring binder is another method of keeping track of your research. Binders work especially well for research from sources other than books and magazines. If you conduct an interview, you can simply three-hole punch your interview notes and put them in the binder. You can print out pages from Internet sources, highlight or underline interesting information, and three-hole punch the pages for your binder.

It's easy to organize your research by creating different sections in your binder with tab dividers. You can create a section that matches each section of your paper, including a "works cited" section that will list all the resources you use in your research.

Advantages and Disadvantages of Three-Ring Binders. Three-ring binders work really well when you are doing most of your research online. Pages printed from the Internet are easy to handle in a three-ring binder. Highlighting information on the printouts may save you time over writing out notes on note cards.

Photocopying pages is a great way to keep track of sources and avoid plagiarism. While many schools can't accommodate photocopying, most public libraries have copiers students can use.

Pages in a binder may not be as easy to manipulate as note cards. However, you can still easily move pages from one section to another.

More Tips and Tricks for Compiling Research:

- As soon as you select a source for research, write down all the information needed for your works cited page. It is very annoying and time-consuming to have to relocate a source online or return to the library to get source information.
- Every single time you take a note or copy a direct quotation—every single time!—write down the source of the information. (For example, "#2, pages 16-17" would refer to information from source #2.)
- When writing an exact quotation, always double-check your work. It is amazing how easy it is to omit something significant or inadvertently change information.
- Immediately put quotation marks around anything you copy word-for-word.
- If you are taking notes using a computer, never, ever copy and paste information from a web site into your notes. It is too easy to wind up plagiarizing, even if you don't mean to.

Taking Notes

Taking notes is not as easy as it sounds. Writers have to manage to get all of the information they need without committing plagiarism. Plagiarism is simply the act of claiming someone else's work or ideas as your own. It is quite easy to accidentally commit plagiarism. (For more information on plagiarism, see pages 55-56.)

Here are some tips for taking notes:

- If you copy a passage word-for-word, be sure to put quotation marks around what you copy. Do this *while* you are taking notes. Then you will know how to handle the passage later, if you use it. If you use a direct quotation, you must tell the source of that quotation.

- Read a few pages from a book, an entire magazine article, or a complete section of a web site *before* you actually start to take notes. Reading first will help you to understand the information, which will make it easier to write about it in your own words. If you start taking notes as you read, you are more likely to merely copy someone else's information without understanding it.

- Don't take notes on something you don't understand. If you can't understand it, it doesn't really belong in your paper.

- Close your source before you take notes. After you finish reading a few paragraphs from a book, for example, close the book. Take out a clean piece of paper or a note card. Write a summary of the information you just read, including only the information you are likely to use later. Don't worry about how to spell things. When you are finished writing, you can open the book to check spelling.

- Reread what you have written. Open your book and skim over the original text to make sure you haven't made any glaring errors in your summary.

- Check to be sure you have noted the page numbers where you found the information, and the source.

- Open your book, and read another section. Then close it and summarize again. The number of times you do this will depend on the length and the complexity of the material. Of course, if you are skimming many paragraphs that have nothing to do with your topic, don't take notes!

Practice

Before you begin doing research and taking notes for your own paper, practice with the excerpt from a magazine article on the next page. Imagine that you are writing a paper with the thesis, "Wal-Mart is good for small-town America." Read the entire excerpt first. Then complete the following:

(continued)

1. First, write a brief summary of the excerpt, in your own words.
2. Then make a note about a direct quotation that might be useful for your paper. (Remember: the point of your paper is that Wal-Mart is *good* for small-town America. Pick a quote that is appropriate.)
3. Reword another item from the excerpt that might be useful for your paper.

The Wal-Mart Effect

Dawn DiPrince, *Blue Sky Quarterly*, Summer 2004. Reprinted with permission.

The term Wal-Mart Effect was coined by economists to describe the monumental ways that the mega-store is transforming both our national and local economies. For example, some economists credit Wal-Mart's low prices with suppressing inflation. Experts also claim Wal-Mart is responsible for increasing productivity rates in our overall economy. (Increased productivity rates were an essential factor in the unfettered economic growth of the 1990s, according to Federal Reserve Chairman Alan Greenspan.)

On the flip side, Wal-Mart's low-price negotiations are credited with hastening the hemorrhage of manufacturing jobs to foreign factories—sometimes Third World sweat shops. Wal-Mart's cost-cutting philosophy is forcing many of its vendors to turn to foreign labor to cut their own production costs. Despite their red, white and blue color scheme and their former "Made in the U.S.A." campaign, more than 85% of Wal-Mart's merchandise is made overseas.

Because Wal-Mart is a giant in size and reach, their every move has implications throughout our economy. Every week, according to Wal-Mart, 138 million customers shop at over 4,750 Wal-Mart stores and supercenters. In 2002, Wal-Mart's "everyday low prices" saved its customers $20 billion. American people buy 30% of their household staples, like toothpaste and paper towels, at Wal-Mart.

At the local level, Wal-Mart is often blamed for the demise of small-town Main Street. To be fair, rural counties across the Great Plains have suffered a long-term population decline since the 1950s, an average loss of 13.6% over four decades. It is more likely the combination of rural decline and Wal-Mart that has created the economic domino effect that begins with the closing of small retail businesses and eventually leads to the closure of other businesses. This sometimes makes Wal-Mart the only retail option for miles. This concentration of retail business creates a major blow for some rural counties, especially those rural counties *without* a Wal-Mart. Their sales tax revenues move to adjacent counties that do have a Wal-Mart.

To see the difference Wal-Mart has made on small rural towns, one only has to peek at a community. Small-town America used to mirror the quaint beauty of a Norman Rockwell painting. Now, these same towns are dotted with boarded-up buildings and strips of empty big box stores. Big box stores like Wal-Mart erect large buildings with specific requirements for their business.

After Wal-Mart leaves a site, they claim to try to sell the building. However, only other mega-stores are generally interested in the super-sized buildings, and Wal-Mart won't sell to its competitors. As of 2000, Wal-Mart has abandoned more than 25 million square feet of retail space across the country. Both urban and rural areas strive for solutions to this empty box store problem.

The Wal-Mart Effect on job creation is also up for debate. Many credit the company with creating jobs. However, a community loses three jobs for every two jobs created by Wal-Mart, according to a Congressional Research Report. These same Wal-Mart jobs are attributed with a decrease in the middle class and an increase in the class of the working poor. In 2001, according to a lawsuit, Wal-Mart associates earned an average of $8.23 an hour, which computes to $13,861 a year. To put this in perspective, the federal poverty guideline is $18,400 for a family of four.

The Wal-Mart Effect has made the store both the most admired and most despised company in America. In 2003 and 2004, *Fortune* magazine deemed the company the Most Admired Company in America. However, over 100 communities each year pool resources to keep the retail giant out of their back yards.

Interviewing

$\mathcal{G}$f you ever watch TV news programs, you know that reporters don't quote the Encyclopedia Britannica. If Wolf Blitzer is reporting on an election in France, he interviews President Nicolas Sarkozy or another French official. He doesn't quote from the "F" volume of an encyclopedia. Because he goes right to the source, his story is more likely to be fresh and interesting.

While you aren't likely to land an interview with Nicolas Sarkozy, you can receive the same benefits as CNN by including interviews in your persuasive paper. Interviews are one of the best tools for finding evidence to support your thesis.

First of all, interviews make your writing as current as possible. While the publishers of encyclopedias work hard at being current, it still takes a couple of years to get a new edition into print. Details can change in that time frame. Interviews can provide you with up-to-the-minute information.

Interviews also give you the ability to learn things you can't learn in a book. For example, if you are looking for information about a certain school policy, you are more likely to get that information from the school principal than from a book.

Finally, interviews give you *primary* information instead of *secondary* information. Primary information is more reliable. (Think about the difference between primary information and secondary information in everyday life. If Zach tells you that Kaci got in trouble for cheating on a test, that is secondary information. If Kaci herself tells you that she got in trouble for cheating, that is primary information. Of course, the story is more believable when it comes directly from Kaci.)

A persuasive paper is usually strengthened when you include an interview. Most communities have experts on a variety of subjects. For example, one student interviewed a local health department official and a local dermatologist when doing a paper on pimples. Another student interviewed volunteers at local homeless shelters when doing a paper on homelessness. Another student, when writing a paper on after-school programs, found a contact at the state education department and interviewed her via both phone and e-mail.

To Get Started

Conducting an interview for a persuasive paper may seem like an impossible task at first, but it is really very easy. While even Wolf Blitzer would agree that it is necessary to do basic research first, a short interview can often provide you with more fresh and original information than an entire afternoon in the library or on the Internet. Here are the steps to getting an interview:

- Brainstorm a list of people you might interview for your paper. If you are having trouble, ask your teacher and other class members to help you brainstorm. When coming up with possibilities, it is a good idea to shoot for the stars. If you are doing a paper about improving local water quality, you might list your U.S. senators and representatives, state legislators, and city council members. However, don't stop there. Also list anyone else you can think of who might have information on your topic. For example, you might list a scientist at a local community college, a worker at the water purification plant, and a doctor who deals with health issues related to water quality.

- From your list, circle your top three interview possibilities. (Realize that you might not be able to set up an interview with your first choice. That's why you should have at least three choices.)

- Write five questions for each of these three interviewees. Some of the questions may be the same for each. That's fine. After each question, make sure that you leave plenty of room to write answers down. (Have your teacher approve your questions, just to be sure you are on the right track.)

- Once you have five questions, you can contact your interviewees. You may contact them in person, by phone, or by e-mail.

- When you call or meet with someone, it is important that you introduce yourself and explain exactly what you need. Here is an example:

Hello. My name is Caitlyn Stenner. I'm a ninth grader at South High School in Pueblo, Colorado. I'm doing a school paper on the nutrition of school lunch programs. I would like to ask you five questions on this topic for my paper. I wondered when you might have some time to talk with me and answer my questions.

This introduction can be given face-to-face, on the phone, left as a message on voice mail (with your phone number), or via e-mail. It is very important that you contact your interviewees as soon as possible. Do not wait until the day before your paper is due to make contact.

The Actual Interview

When you first contact people about interviews, some may be ready to answer your questions right then. Others may need to schedule another time. (If you do schedule a later time, make sure it is a time you are available. Also, make sure that you don't forget.)

For a successful interview, follow the steps below.

- Before you begin any interview, always ask the person to spell his/her name. Even if his name is Joe Smith, make sure you get the right spelling. (His name could be spelled Jo Smythe.) Also, ask the interviewee to give you his or her exact title, such as principal of Roosevelt High School, or United States Senator and member of the Senate Foreign-Relations Committee.

(continued)

- Then, go ahead and get started. When doing an interview, try to be both quick and thorough. People are busy, so you don't want to waste their time. However, you do want to be accurate. After you ask your question, write down everything you possibly can that your interviewee says. In fact, you might even want to consider taping the interview. (Be sure to ask permission from the interviewee before taping, though.)

    You can abbreviate words in any way that works for you. Be sure that your notes capture the essence of what is said, and the sentiment. For example, suppose your interviewee says, "We donate food every year to the homeless shelter fund-raiser because it is the right thing to do. It also helps to remind us of the struggle of some less fortunate people." Possible notes:

    YES: *Donate food evry yr to hmless shtr bcse rt thing to do. Helps remind us struggle of some people.*

    NO: *right thing to do: struggle*

    It is perfectly all right to ask your interviewee to give you a moment to write things down. People generally don't mind waiting and appreciate your trying to quote them as accurately as possible.

- After you have finished asking your five questions, always ask: "Is there anything else you would like to add?" This is usually the best part of the interview, so don't relax your note taking just yet. Interviewees usually give their best quotes at this point in the interview.

- When you are finished with your questions, thank the interviewee. (Example: "Thank you so much for your time. I know you are busy, and I appreciate it.")

Follow-up

When your actual interview is finished, your work is not. It is essential to go over your notes immediately after an interview. Some professional reporters sit in their cars to do this after an interview because they know the ideas won't be as fresh by the time they get back to the office.

- Go through your notes and write out the words for any abbreviations you may have used in your note taking. Otherwise, you may be confused later on by the abbreviations you have used.

- Right after you have corrected your abbreviations, write a summary of your interview. This doesn't have to be perfect prose. Just write something that will remind you of how someone looked or the tone of voice the person used. Write out answers the person gave, putting quotation marks around any direct quotes. Completing this step makes it easy to insert an interview into your paper later.

- Be sure to send a thank-you note to anyone you interview. (It's fine to do this by e-mail, if you like. Regular mail also works, of course.) In some cases, you may even want to send the person a copy of your finished paper, with your thank you written on the top.

Common Sense Ways
to Battle Plagiarism

Teacher Instructions

According to recent studies, plagiarism is a growing problem in American schools. Donald McCabe, founder of the Center for Academic Integrity, conducted a national survey of high school students in 2001. The study revealed that 72% of those surveyed admitted to serious cheating on written assignments. He also discovered that 54% of surveyed students admitted to stealing material off the Internet. Of those surveyed, 74% engaged in serious cheating in the past school year.

One reason for the increase in cheating is use of the Internet. With web sites like cheathouse.com and MonsterPapers.com, stealing someone else's work has become even easier for students. On the flip side, new web sites like TurnItIn.com and iThenticate.com are cropping up to help teachers in this growing battle.

Despite this high-tech world of cheat and deceit, a little common sense is often the best approach to battling plagiarism. Here are a few low-tech ideas:

- Ask students to defend their work. Without warning, ask a student pointed questions about the ideas conveyed in his paper. Only students who did the actual research and work necessary will be able to answer your questions.

- Be suspicious when a student who usually has trouble writing complete sentences suddenly turns in brilliant prose.

- Ask students to turn in their note cards and/or binders with their papers.

- Play dumb. If a section of a paper seems suspicious, ask a student to show you the source for a statement made in that section. Ask to see a photocopy of the actual page from which the notes were taken. Even students who honestly don't think they have plagiarized can easily be shown their mistakes when you go to the original source.

- Spend some time in class teaching about plagiarism. Students, when armed with the correct information, often don't *mean* to plagiarize.

Plagiarism Quiz

Most students know that plagiarism involves stealing someone else's work and pretending that it is your own. Most also know that it is wrong. That's where the clarity ends. Test your own knowledge of what is and is not plagiarism. Answer *True* or *False* to the questions below.

_____ 1. Plagiarism involves copying something without giving any credit.

_____ 2. Copying information and text from the Internet is not considered plagiarism.

_____ 3. It is not plagiarism if you copy the material yourself, in your own handwriting.

_____ 4. It is possible to plagiarize someone's ideas, even if you don't copy the person's words.

_____ 5. Plagiarism is a crime. Plagiarists can even go to jail.

_____ 6. By law, a person can be fined up to $50,000 for plagiarism.

_____ 7. In some cases, students who plagiarize can flunk class or be expelled from school.

_____ 8. Writing your name on a paper written by someone else and turning it in is wrong, but it is not plagiarism.

_____ 9. Forgetting to put quotation marks around words that someone else said or wrote is an honest mistake and not plagiarism.

_____ 10. When you copy material from another source, changing one or two words is enough to avoid plagiarism.

_____ 11. When you copy word-for-word from another source, it is important to put the words in quotation marks and cite where the information came from.

_____ 12. To avoid plagiarizing, it is important to paraphrase any research in your own words.

_____ 13. You are guilty of plagiarism only when you knowingly copy someone else's work.

_____ 14. You are free to copy any material that does not have a copyright symbol (©) on it.

_____ 15. Teachers have web sites and computer programs that tell them if students have plagiarized or not.

Citing Sources

Citing sources is a writer's best defense against plagiarism. Citing sources simply means to tell where you found material you have included in your work.

Just because material doesn't have a copyright symbol (©) doesn't mean it's not copyrighted. Current copyright law holds that anything a person writes is immediately protected by copyright law, whether or not it uses the copyright symbol.

Why do you need to cite sources? For one thing, copyright laws require you to do so. For another, telling where you found information helps readers know where to go to find out more.

Writers should cite sources when they:

- Use quotes or copy word-for-word from a source.
- Paraphrase or rewrite materials from another source.
- Use ideas expressed by someone else.
- Create ideas that are based on someone else's material or ideas.

Common Knowledge

There is one kind of information you do *not* need to cite when you are using material found in research. That is something called common knowledge. Common knowledge is a body of information that is commonly known and that can be found in a variety of sources. For example, it is common knowledge that penguins live in Antarctica. It is common knowledge that Denver is the capitol of Colorado. It is common knowledge that Julia Roberts was once married to Lyle Lovett. (It doesn't matter that *you* may not know this. It was widely reported at the time, and the information can be found in countless sources.) You would not need to cite a source for any of these bits of knowledge.

You *would* need to cite a source if you quoted a scientist who has a theory about the health of penguins in this century. You would need to cite a source if you gave some statistics about air pollution in Denver. You would need to cite a source if you used information from an in-depth article about Julia Roberts' childhood.

If you are ever in doubt about what is common knowledge and what isn't, play it safe and cite a source.

How to Cite Sources

If you had lived through the olden days of footnotes and typewriters, you would agree that in-text citation is the best thing to happen to English classes since spell check. In-text citation means that you put information about a source in parentheses within your paper, right after you use information from that source.

In the past, students had to cite sources by putting footnotes at the bottom of every page of their papers. Making sure they had enough space at the bottom of the page required a ruler and lots of luck. If they guessed wrong, they often had to start over and type a page again.

In-text citation is endorsed by the Modern Language Association (MLA), a group started in 1883 by teachers and scholars to promote the study of language and literature. This association literally wrote the book on how to write and document student papers. Its guidebook includes everything from selecting a topic to submitting a completed paper.

Using the MLA form, in-text citations are simple.

Step One—Within a Paper

To give credit to a source in your paper, put in parentheses the author's last name and the page number(s) where you found the information you are citing.

Example:

Most people have heard the saying, "A rose by any other name would smell as sweet" (Shakespeare 45).

If you can't find the author's name, use the title of the work instead of the author's name.

Example:

Some experts believe that Shakespeare may not have written all of the plays that carry his name ("No Fear Shakespeare" 37).

Punctuating in-text citations is simple. Put the parentheses before the end punctuation in the sentence. Do not use any punctuation between the author's name and the page number.

Step Two—At the End of a Paper

A works cited page is a separate page at the end of your paper. It includes all of the information about every book, magazine article, web page, etc., used in your research. Here's an example of one entry on a works cited page:

Stewart, Jon. *The Daily Show with Jon Stewart Presents America (The Book): A Citizen's Guide to Democracy Inaction.* New York City: Warner Books, 2004.

For more detailed information about the correct way to list everything from web pages to poems to television programs, it is important to consult the *MLA Handbook for Writers of Research Papers* or one of many online references like Purdue's Online Writing lab (OWL): http://owl.english.purdue.edu/.

Tips for Writing the Body

Arguing Your Point Effectively

The body is the foundation of any persuasive paper. This is where writers have to roll up their sleeves and get to the nitty-gritty of making their argument. Writers have to juggle research and evidence with strong writing, and they have to tie it neatly together with solid transitions. This section gives student writers practice in synthesizing information, writing transitions, using a convincing voice and examining the opposite views.

Think Elbows!

Your elbow does have a purpose beyond jabbing friends when you want them to notice something. It joins the top of your arm with the bottom of your arm, connecting the two parts in a way that allows your arm to work better. Our arms would not function very well without the connection created by elbows.

Sentences and paragraphs need connections, too. When you write, *transition words* help connect different thoughts and make your writing flow more smoothly. *Transition words* bring thoughts, sentences and paragraphs together into one coherent piece. Without them, each thought can seem to flail alone.

Transition words are important in all kinds of writing, but they are especially important in persuasive writing. The point of persuasive writing is to make a good argument, and transition words help you lead readers in the direction you want to take them.

Consider these two examples:

No transitions. *Student lockers are school property. They contain a student's personal items. Student lockers should be protected by privacy laws.*

With transitions. *Although student lockers are school property, they contain a student's personal items. Therefore, student lockers should be protected by privacy laws.*

The first example is very choppy. The second flows better and is easier to understand.

Practice

Add transition words from the box below to the choppy sentences on the next page. Use the transition words to help make the sentences flow more smoothly and make better sense.

Transition Words

and • but • or • while • although • unlike • however • yet
unless • therefore • in contrast • similarly • in other words
to sum up • because • consequently • first • next • sometimes
surely • besides • undoubtedly • in addition • likewise • furthermore
for instance • on the other hand

(continued)

1. The room I share with my sister is wallpapered with Nelly posters. I can't stand Nelly. The posters should come down.

2. Many adults argue that teenagers watch too much television. Most teenagers have responsibilities like work, homework, sports practice, music lessons or play practice. Teenagers don't have time to watch too much television.

3. I am a hard worker and good student. I am responsible and enthusiastic. I am a not-so-nerdy bookworm. The Thurgood Marshall Public Library should hire me for the summer.

4. Phoenix Suns' player Shaquille O'Neal is over 7 feet tall. He is one of the biggest players in the NBA. Shaquille O'Neal is one of the top ranked players in the sport. Shaquille O'Neal can't make his free throws.

5. I think that eggs, waffles and Pop Tarts are gross. Bacon, cinnamon toast and grapefruit halves are disgusting. I can't find any breakfast food I would want to choke down. I usually prefer to skip breakfast.

Connecting Paragraphs

Many students think that paragraphs are just five or six sentences grouped together. While paragraphs do contain sentences, they are much more than that. Paragraphs are a group of sentences that all address the same idea. When you change the idea you are writing about, you should start a new paragraph.

The trick, however, is to make all your different paragraphs connect and hang together. That is where transition words come in. Amazingly, these little words and phrases can make the difference between a coherent, organized paper and a confusing, jumbled paper.

Practice

Take a look at how professional writers use transitions. Comb through magazine and newspaper articles, hunting for transitional words or phrases.

Collect three news articles and circle all of the transition words in each article. To help you remember, refer to the transition words in the box below.

Transition Words

and • but • or • although • unlike • while • however • yet
unless • therefore • in contrast • similarly • in other words
to sum up • because • consequently • first • next • sometimes
surely • besides • undoubtedly • in addition • likewise • furthermore
for instance • on the other hand •

Follow-up

Read each article to yourself *without* the circled transition words. Read each article with the transition words. In a sentence or two, describe the difference. How do transitions improve writing?

Synthesizing Information

Of you have ever heard a song re-mix, you know what synthesizing is. Synthesizing is taking items from different places and weaving them together in a cohesive way. While it sounds easy enough, synthesizing your own ideas with what you have found in research can be difficult. It involves weaving information from several or many different places into one coherent thought.

Directions

Practice your synthesizing ability by molding all of the information below into one paragraph. Remember, transitions are key to making your thoughts flow smoothly. Use the common transition words in the box below to help you.

Transition *Words*

and • but • or •although • unlike •while • however •yet • unless • therefore
in contrast • similarly •because • in other words • to sum up • consequently
first • next • sometimes • surely • besides • undoubtedly •in addition • likewise
furthermore • for instance • on the other hand

Main Point: *More and more children and families are suffering from hunger every year.*

Evidence: *Poverty rates are on the rise, according to census information compiled by Second Harvest, a nonprofit food bank network.*

"Between 2000 and 2001, poverty rose to 11.7% of the population, or 32.9 million people, up from 11.3% and 31.6 million," says America's Second Harvest.

According to their own study, food banks across the country have had an 86% increase in requests for food assistance over the past year.

A "food insecure" household is a household that does not always have enough food for an active, healthy life.

According to a report by the USDA, 14.8% of American households with children were "food insecure." That rate rose to 16.1% in 2001.

Ethos, Pathos & Logos

What are *ethos, pathos* and *logos*? They are not the names of the Three Musketeers or the Three Stooges. *Ethos, pathos* and *logos* are the three "modes of persuasion," according to Aristotle. Every persuasive argument, either in writing or in speech, should include all three.

But what exactly *are* they? Read on.

Ethos, a Greek word, is the basis for the English word "ethics." The term *ethics* refers to principles of right and wrong. While it is important to engage in ethical arguments, *ethos* involves much more than that. Ethos relates to the writer. When writing a persuasive paper, the writer must appear trustworthy and honest. In order to have a reader listen to an argument, the writer must be believable.

How can you show readers you are trustworthy when writing your argument? There are several ways. First of all, it is important not to use overblown language, or words that exaggerate the truth. For example, if 25 quiet protesters demonstrated at the state capitol building, you shouldn't report that *a horde of angry militants stormed the capitol steps.*

One of the best ways to get readers to listen to your perspective is to show them that you have considered the other point of view. A writer is more believable when you know he or she has judged both sides of an issue. You may want to acknowledge any good arguments that support the opposing point of view. This gives you an opportunity to point out any flaws in these arguments, or to explain how your arguments outweigh those for the other side.

Pathos stands for emotion. Every good argument appeals to the emotions. Have you ever felt like crying during a commercial that shows hungry children or a teenager killed by a drunk driver? Such commercials try to persuade us with images and stories that tug at our emotions.

Facts and statistics can make a good argument, but they are dry and dull without pathos. For example, a paper on homelessness is probably much more effective if you include a story about the experiences of a homeless 13-year-old. A paper on Alzheimer's disease may be much more effective if you include a story about your own grandfather's struggle with the disease.

Logos is about logic. Logos represents the part of the argument based on reason, solid facts and sound information. It is the foundation of a good argument. You can't have ethos in an argument without good logos. Logos is also important to the pathos part of your argument. It will seem overly sentimental if you can't back it up with logos.

The best way to include logos in your argument is by having three strong *reasons why* to back up your point of view. Then back up these reasons why by including some or all of the following: facts, expert opinions, statistics, examples, and/or anecdotes.

(continued)

Directions

Letters that make a request are a form of persuasive writing. For example, the following letter includes *ethos*, *pathos* and *logos*. Find an example of each.

Dear Santa:

Last year you made my Christmas very happy by bringing me an adorable, fluffy white kitty. As I'm sure you know, because you can see everything, I named my kitty Pancho. Pancho and I were the best of friends, especially since I don't have too many people friends. She and I did everything together, or at least until mean old Brady Pilger from down the street ran over Pancho while speeding in his truck with monster wheels.

As I'm sure you already know, I am a good person. Dr. Berry, my physics teacher, always says, "Crystal is such a good kid. I wish there were more like her." I also was a loving friend to Pancho. I hope that this year for Christmas you can bring me another fluffy white kitty, since I know that Pancho will never come back.

Besides wanting a new friend, I am a responsible cat owner. I walked Pancho every day and will do the same with any new kitty. I also believe in cleaning litter boxes every day and feeding cats healthy wet food from Science Diet. I will brush any new kitty's fur every single day and keep her claws neatly trimmed. Santa, I think you can clearly see that I would be an excellent candidate for a new kitty.

Thank you,
Crystal Puddles

Write a persuasive letter on one of the following subjects. Be sure your letter includes *ethos*, *pathos* and *logos*:

- Write to a local pet shop, asking for a refund for your turtle Marigold who died only 10 days after you bought her.
- Write a letter to your favorite singer, QueAreEss, asking him to visit your hometown.
- Write to the Queen of England, asking that the Buckingham Palace Guard stop using real bear fur in their uniform hats.

UNDERLINE EACH of YOUR THREE EXAMPLES

Effective Evidence

Evidence for your persuasive paper can come in a variety of different forms. Here are some common forms of evidence:

Facts. Facts bolster your argument because they can be confirmed or verified. Someone can try to argue that George Washington wasn't the first U.S. President, but hundreds of history books will confirm that he was.

Expert opinion. Although you can't use your own opinion as evidence in a paper, it *is* acceptable to use an expert's. The trick is that you need to make sure the "expert" is indeed an expert. For example, for a paper on the toxic effects of caffeine, you might quote a neurologist who has studied the effects of caffeine on the brain. You should not quote your Auntie Sally just because she is really healthy.

Statistics. According to some studies, five out of every six people are convinced by statistics.

Are you convinced? You shouldn't be. The statistic above was simply made up to illustrate that statistics can be quite convincing.

Statistics are basically the numbers behind your topic. They can be based on census data, polls, survey information, scientific studies, etc. Statistics are very useful, but it is important to look at them carefully and check their source. Statistics can be easily manipulated. All too often, people can cite convincing statistics on both sides of an issue.

Example. Examples illustrate the point you are making. They help make theories and ideas concrete and understandable.

Suppose you write that a fiber-optic network moves information at the speed of 100 megabytes (MB) per second. You might then use an example like this: *To give you a sense of that kind of speed, imagine a computer floppy disk. There are 1.4 MB on a regular floppy. A fiber optic network is the equivalent of over 70 diskettes moving from computer to computer each second!*

Anecdote. Anecdotes are stories based on your own experiences or those of people you know or have read about. For example, if you are writing about the dangers of pit bulls, you may want to interview the mother of a toddler who was attacked by one. Telling her family's story in your paper could powerfully illustrate your point.

Passing the RAD test

All evidence used in a persuasive paper should be Relevant, Accurate and Detailed.

Relevant means that the evidence fits the argument you are making. For example, you don't want statistics on childhood obesity when you are writing a paper on childhood hunger.

Accurate simply means that you are precisely and correctly conveying your facts. All evidence should be accurate. For example, when you quote someone in your paper, you must quote them exactly. You can't fudge their statement to make it fit your argument better.

Detailed evidence is more accurate than vague information. Details can also be more compelling. For example, it is more effective to say, "Ten million moms marched on Washington," than "Some women marched on Washington."

Directions

Magazine and online articles effectively use the above types of evidence. Find an example of each. (You might even get lucky and find all examples in one article.)

For *and* Against

Have you ever been guilty of arguing just to argue? Perhaps your mother told you your pants are too baggy. Since you must keep a finger laced in your belt loop just to keep your pants on, you know that she is right. However, for some reason, you don't want your mother to be right about anything, so you argue that your pants are just right.

When mastering the art of persuasion, arguing for the sake of arguing can help you learn to see both sides of an issue. Seeing both sides is important, if only to help you anticipate arguments others might make.

Directions:

Choose one of the topics below and write one paragraph "for" the issue and one paragraph "against" the issue. Be as convincing as possible for both sides of the argument.

- Schools should not be co-ed. Girls should go to all-girl schools, and boys should go to all-boy schools.
- Children should be paid for doing household chores.
- Children should be allowed to watch no more than a half hour of television per day.
- Every child should take music lessons for at least one year.
- Every child should have a pet.

The Rebuttal

While it is important to mention opinions from the other side of an issue in your persuasive paper, it is equally important to "rebut" those opinions. In other words, you should tell what the other side thinks and then go on to tell what is wrong with that point of view.

A useful tool for a rebuttal is the "comma but" sentence. With a "comma but" sentence, you mention an opposing view and then, after a comma and a "but," refute it. Here's an example:

Some experts believe that a low-carb diet is healthy, but the American Heart Association still recommends a low-fat diet as the best way to stay healthy.

A "comma but" is not the only option you have, of course. Transition words are the key to a good rebuttal statement. Here's an example:

While many people purchase animals at a pet store, it is much more compassionate to adopt an animal from your local Humane Society.

"While" is the transition used in this rebuttal statement.

Directions

Combine each of the pairs of sentences below to create a clear, one sentence rebuttal. Use a different transition for each rebuttal. (The transition box on the right can help you.) The first one is done for you.

1. Tanya has a huge crush on Ryan Seacrest. I think he is lame.

   Although Tanya has a huge crush on Ryan Seacrest, I think he is lame.

2. Some people are crazy about a Starbucks Mochachino. I prefer to stick with skinny lattes.

3. A vegetarian diet is probably better for you. I could never give up triple threat meatball sandwiches.

4. Mom says it would look tacky to get my nose pierced. I think it would look elegant.

5. Everyone I know wants a big monster SUV. My dream car is a little purple Saturn.

Transition Words

and • but • or
while • although
unlike • yet
however • unless
therefore • first
in contrast • similarly
because • next
in other words
to sum up
consequently
sometimes • surely
besides • undoubtedly
in addition • likewise
furthermore
for instance
on the other hand

I Feel Wishy-Washy

Imagine that a teacher is giving you advice about persuasive writing. Which of the following versions sounds more convincing?

> When you are writing a persuasive paper, I think that you should not use these phrases: "I think," "I feel," or "I believe." I feel that these phrases make you sound wishy-washy. I believe that your opinion is stronger when you leave them out.

OR

> When you are writing a persuasive paper, do not use the phrases "I think," "I feel," or "I believe." These phrases make you sound wishy-washy. Your opinion is stronger when you leave them out.

The second version, of course, is much stronger.

When they are trying to make a point, many people throw in phrases like *I think, I feel,* or *I believe.* They sometimes believe that such words make them sound more polite. They actually make them sound less certain. Leaving out such phrases allows an opinion to stand out more clearly.

Think about it. What if Thomas Jefferson had written "I think that all men are created equal"? It just doesn't pack the same punch as "All men are created equal."

Directions

Rewrite the e-mail letter below, taking out all of the wishy-washy phrases like *I think, I feel,* or *I believe.* (You may have to take out the word *that* sometimes, too.)

Dear gooeylouie@hotmail.com:

Eddie, I think that you are the one for me, and I believe that I am the one for you. I think that you are always looking at me in Mrs. Dietz's class. I feel we are a match made in heaven. Even though you are always in in-school suspension, I believe that you are a good person deep down inside. My mom and my best friend Shelby don't agree, but I think that they just don't know you like I do. I think that we should declare our love to the whole school by going to the Fall Festival together. What do you think?
Love,
diamondprincess4567@yahoo.com (Clarissa)

Follow-up

Write a strong, opinionated e-mail from Shelby to Clarissa, persuading her to stop chasing Eddie. Remember, do not include phrases like *I think, I believe,* or *I feel.*

Kind of . . . Sort of

When former Austrian weight lifter Arnold Schwarzenegger ran for governor of California, no one heard him say, "I kind of want to be governor of California. I'm sort of the man for the job."

Like most successful politicians, Schwarzenegger knew that words like *kind of* and *sort of* sound wimpy and ineffective. He was much more likely to say, "I want to be governor of California. I'm the man for the job."

Like Schwarzenegger, your persuasive writing should be strong. Just adding the words "kind of" or "sort of" make your argument seem more like Stuart Little than Arnold Schwarzenegger.

Directions

Your best friend Jody isn't ready to run for governor, but she is ready to run for president of your school's student council. On a separate sheet of paper, help her make her speech stronger and more effective by taking out all the "wimpy" words and phrases:

Principal Gomez, teachers, students, and honored guests:
I kind of want to talk to you about my qualifications for student council president. I think that I would be more or less the best person for the job because I sort of love this school. Don't you kind of agree that a student council president should feel sort of strongly about her school? I also feel that I'm pretty qualified because I'm kind of a good student. I've also served on student council for the past two years, so I sort of know how everything works. So, if you love this school, like I sort of do, then I think you should vote for me, if you want. Thank you.

Follow-up

After hearing Jody's wishy-washy speech, you decide to run for student council president yourself. Write a speech explaining in strong language why your fellow students should vote for *you*.

Writing an Introduction and a Conclusion
Ideas for Beginnings and Endings

While the body is the foundation of any persuasive paper, the introduction and the conclusion are critically important in making an argument. Although there are many approaches to writing introductions and conclusions, this section outlines some practical ideas and step-by-step instructions.

While it is possible to write the introduction before starting the body of a paper, many people find it more effective to write the introduction *after* they write the body of their paper. That way they know the actual content of the paper and avoid the "How to begin?" paralysis that can affect many writers.

Starting Steps for an Introduction

Two wrestlers enter the arena with music, lights and much fanfare. When they reach the wrestling ring, they remove their silky robes, revealing glitzy outfits. After the official blows the start whistle, the two wrestlers dance around the edge and scowl at each other. Only after all of this do the wrestlers finally pounce on each other, and the match begins.

In some ways, the introduction to a persuasive paper is very similar to a professional wrestling match. A lot goes on before the first "punch." You must announce yourself and dance a little before you can deliver your message.

The introduction acts as an attention-getting device. It tells readers, "Hey, pay attention to what I have to say!" It also serves as a road map to the rest of your paper because it includes the main "punch"—your thesis statement.

Many writers have a hard time writing introductions. For some help getting started, complete the steps below. You will be gathering information for your introduction with these steps, *not* writing the actual introduction.

Later you will use the information you have gathered to try two different methods of writing a strong introduction.

The Glitz

The first part of an introduction is "the glitz." You should begin in a way that grabs the reader's attention—perhaps with a powerful quote, a strong statement, or a bold statistic. Follow the steps below to gather information for this part of your introduction.

1. Find a quotation that fits your topic. Look for something by a famous person or expert. Consult a book of quotations, or visit a web site like *www.bartleby.com* to search for one. Make sure your quotation is both gripping and relevant to your argument. Here is an example of a quotation from an introduction to a paper on childhood hunger:

    "Children often constitute a large part of the face of hunger and homelessness in our country," says Marian Wright Edelman, founder of the Children's Defense Fund.

    For some papers, it might be appropriate to quote someone who is not famous, but who is significant to your argument. For example, a paper on childhood hunger might use this quotation:

    "When you're hungry, you can't think about anything else," says seven-year-old Sarah.

    (continued)

Write a quotation for your introduction in the space below:

2. Find statistics that are relevant to your topic. For a paper on childhood hunger, for example, you might write:

    Every day over 13 million children in the United States don't know where their next meal is coming from, according to America's Second Harvest.

    Notice that this example tells where the statistics came from. Never, ever use statistics without telling their source.

    Write your statistics in the space below.

3. Write a bold statement about your topic here. You might use the declaration you have already written, or a form of it. Or you might write something new. Here's an example of a bold statement you might use for a paper on childhood hunger:

    While every grocery story in America is bursting with an overwhelming amount of food, children in our country still go to bed hungry.

    Write your bold statement in the space below:

The Dance

The next part of your introduction is "the dance." In a few sentences, you size up your argument, just as a wrestler sizes up his opponent. You give information that leads into the argument you are going to be making. Follow the steps below to gather information for this part of your introduction.

1. Write three facts about your topic. These might be facts you learned in your research or facts that you already knew. They should not be facts mentioned in the steps above.

(continued)

Write your facts here:

2. Write three more ideas you would like to convey about your topic. Feel free to write whatever comes to mind, including some of your opinions.

The Punch

The final part of your introduction is where you land your first punch. English teachers like to call this first punch a thesis statement. A thesis statement lays out your argument with a big wallop. With strong language, you begin a strong argument. Finally, write the complete thesis statement you developed earlier for your paper. If you need to make any changes to it because of what you have learned in your research, now is the time.

Write your thesis statement here:

Putting It Together
Version #1

Now that you have completed "The Glitz," "The Dance," and "The Punch" steps, you are ready to begin writing your introduction. Although there are many ways to write an introduction, this exercise will show you one simple way. Just complete the sections below, using the information you have already gathered.

The Glitz. Choose one of your items from "The Glitz"—the quotation, the statistics, or the bold statement. Use it to begin your introduction. Example:

"When you're hungry, you can't think about anything else," says seven-year-old Sarah.

The Dance. Follow up with three to five sentences based on your information from "The Dance." Example:

According to America's Second Harvest, Sarah is just one of the over 13 million children in the United States who don't know if or when they will get their next meal. Since the U.S. is the richest country in the world, it is surprising that so many American children suffer from hunger. Childhood hunger also violates our ideals that everyone has the right to life, liberty and the pursuit of happiness.

The Punch. Write your thesis statement next. Example:

It is our moral duty to protect U.S. children from hunger because they are innocent, this country has so much, and they are our future.

The Complete Introduction. Next, compile all three items above into one paragraph. You may need to add transitional words to make the paragraph flow better. Example:

"When you are hungry, you can't think about anything else," says seven-year-old Sarah. Sarah is just one of the over 13 million children in the United States, according to America's Second Harvest, who don't know if or when they will get their next meal. Since the U.S. is the richest country in the world, it is surprising that so many American children suffer from hunger. Childhood hunger also violates our ideals that everyone has the right to life, liberty and the pursuit of happiness. It is our moral duty to protect U.S. children from hunger because they are innocent, this country has so much, and they are our future.

After you are finished proofreading and revising, you have the first paragraph of your persuasive paper—your introduction.

Putting It Together
Version #2

Another approach to writing an introduction allows a writer more freedom and can produce more interesting writing. Try this approach to see if it fits you better.

Review. Read over and think about what you wrote in gathering information for "The Glitz," "The Dance," and "The Punch."

Choose an Opening Line. Choose an opening line you like from "The Glitz." Write that sentence at the top of a separate sheet of paper.

Freewrite. Using the sentence you just wrote as your opening line, set a timer and freewrite for five minutes. Follow these rules:

- **Don't stop.** Write continuously. Don't lift your pencil or pen from the paper.
- **Don't erase.** Later, you can correct anything you don't like.
- **Don't read over what you are writing.** You can read over what you've written after the timer rings.
- **Don't worry about spelling.** Circle misspelled words so you can go back and fix them later.
- **Leave a blank if you can't think of a word you want.** You can fill in the word later.
- **Don't be afraid to start over.** If you lose your train of thought or run out of ideas before the timer rings, start over from the beginning.

Read over what you've written immediately after time is up. That way you can easily fill in gaps, fix words, and make changes while your thoughts are still fresh.

Add Your Thesis Statement. If you haven't done so already, write your thesis statement at the end of your freewriting.

Revise. Use what you have written during freewriting as the basis for your introduction. Think carefully as you revise it. Did you include all of the ideas you wanted? Is there anything in your paragraph that doesn't belong? Take out extra words, or add new details.

The result should be a good first draft of your introduction.

The Conclusion Formula

Writing a conclusion is generally the easiest and most boring step in finishing a persuasive paper. However, it is a very important step. The conclusion is the last thing readers will remember about your argument. It needs to tie up your ideas into a nicely summarized little package and also leave the reader with something to think about.

The conclusion is not the place to introduce new arguments. It should only review points you have already made.

Most conclusions follow a fairly standard formula. A conclusion includes the following:

- Your declaration
- Your *reasons why*
- Something to think about

Look at the "Conclusion Formula" below.

Conclusion Formula

Clearly, music sharing on the Internet is good for music.
_____
(Transition) ,   (Your declaration)

First of all, it takes music out of big business and gives it back to musicians and listeners.
_____
(Transition) ,   (First "reason why")

Secondly, music has always been created by borrowing from other songs.
_____
(Transition) ,   (Second "reason why")

Finally, music sharing online offers more musicians the opportunity to reach an audience.
_____
(Transition) ,   (Third "reason why")

While the music industry believes the free flow of music online is bad for music, the opposite is true. The Internet offers a creative playing field where more music can be created, shared, and enjoyed by people all over the world.
_____
(Something to think about)

Note: Each of the items above can include one or two sentences.

(continued)

Now it is your turn. Use the form below to help you write the conclusion for your own persuasive paper.

Your Declaration

Transition: _____   Your declaration: _____

_____

_____

Your Reasons Why

Transition: _____   First reason why: _____

_____

_____

Transition: _____   Second reason why: _____

_____

_____

Transition: _____   Third reason why: _____

_____

_____

Something to Think About

Something to think about: _____

_____

_____

You now have a rough draft of your conclusion. All you need to do now is revise and proofread.

Answer Keys

Possible Responses

Point of View, page 10

Answers will vary. Here is one possibility:

Little Red Riding Hood

One day my mom tells me that grandma is sick and I have to take some food to her at her place on the other side of the forest. I put on my red cape and head out. It feels pretty cool skipping down the path in the woods. But suddenly this horrible wolf jumps out at me and says, "Where are you off to, little girl?"

Well, I don't feel much like talking to a wolf, but I figure I don't have a lot of choice. So I say, "Grandma's. She's not feeling well."

So this wolf says, "I think I will go and visit her to make her feel better. Say, why don't we have a race to see who can get there first?"

I agree. I mean, what choice do I have? Then I watch him vanish into the forest. I laugh because the stupid wolf runs off in the wrong direction.

I go on to Grandma's and knock on the door. Grandma yells, "Come in, dear!" I stop in my tracks. She looks terrible!

"Grandma," I say. "You don't look so good. What big ears you have!"

"Only to hear you better with, my dear," she says.

"And what big eyes you have!"

"The better to see you with."

"And what big teeth you have!"

"The better to eat you with, my dear!" Grandma growls back. Well, I'll tell you, *that* sure surprises me. But worse, Grandma leaps off the bed at me! Finally, I figure it out. It's not Grandma. It's the wolf, dressed up like Grandma! He opens his jaws and swallows me in one bite! It's hard to believe, but I join Grandma in his belly. For a long time, Grandma and me listen to the wolf's loud snores.

Then we hear a loud crash and see the blades of Grandma's sewing scissors poke through the wolf's stomach. We're saved! We get out of that belly, *fast!* We see this guy standing there, and he tells us to gather rocks to put in the wolf's stomach. It's a weird request, but we do it, and Grandma sews up the wolf's stomach. Then the three of us go outside and hide.

We hear a giant burp from the cottage and the wolf stumbles out. He mumbles something to himself and disappears into the forest. I sure hope it's forever!

The Wolf

My stomach is growling again, I'm so darned hungry. The good eats in this forest have been hard to find lately.

Suddenly I hear someone coming down the path. It's this girl in a red hood, skipping down the trail. I want to get her to stop, so I act real friendly. "Hello, little girl. Where are you off to this fine day?" I ask.

"Grandma's," she says. "She's not feeling well."

"Oh," I say. "I think I will go and visit her to make her feel better. Say, why don't we have a race to see who can get there first?" The little girl doesn't look too thrilled about it, but she agrees, and so I turn around and head off into the forest. I know a shortcut.

Because I know a shortcut, I get to Grandma's place before the girl. I knock on the door and Grandma yells for "Little Red Riding Hood" to come in. I rush in and swallow her in one gulp before she knows what happened. Yum! I feel full at last—but not full enough to pass up another treat. I quickly put on one of Grandma's nightgowns and a bed cap and get into her bed.

The little girl in the red cape gets there and I tell her to come in. I do a pretty good imitation of an old lady, if I do say so myself! The girl crosses the room and leans over to look at her grandma.

"Grandma, you don't look so good," she says. "What big ears you have."

"Only to hear you better with, my dear."

"And what big eyes you have!"

"The better to see you with."

"What big teeth you have!"

"The better to eat you with, my dear!" I jump on her and swallow her in one gulp. Now I feel great! I haven't been this full in weeks!

I doze off for some time and when I wake up, there's an awful pain in my belly. I just don't understand it. I go outside to walk off the pain, but it doesn't help. "I must be getting old," I think to myself. "I can't even eat a little girl and her grandma without feeling as though my belly is full of stones!"

I don't think I'll ever eat humans again. They just don't agree with me.

Grandma

When I hear the knock at my door, I know it's my darling Little Red Riding Hood, at last. "Come in, Little Red Riding Hood!" I shout from my bed.

Just then something hits me with such force that everything goes dark. It isn't until later that I realize what has happened. A wolf has come in and swallowed me whole! I wasn't feeling well before. Well, you can imagine how I feel now! I'm in a wolf's belly, for heaven's sake!

From inside the belly, I hear another knock on the door. In no time at all, here comes my granddaughter sliding down the wolf's throat. She shakes with fear and we both start to cry. It seems like hours go by as we sit there crying and shaking with fear, listening to the loud rumble of the wolf snoring.

Suddenly I hear the front door crash open. Then we see the shiny blades of my sewing scissors slicing through the wolf's stomach. Hallelujah! We are free! We climb out and see a woodcutter standing in my cottage. Is he ever a sight for sore eyes! We thank him and thank him and thank him, and then he tells us to gather stones to put in the wolf's stomach. I sew up the wolf's stomach and we run outside to hide until the wolf wakes up. We have to see what happens.

We hear a giant burp from the cottage and the wolf stumbles out. He mumbles something to himself and disappears into the forest. I hope he has a really bad case of indigestion!

The Woodcutter

See, I'm on my way home when I hear the sound of snoring from a cottage. Well, I would recognize that snore anywhere. It's the big bad wolf! What the heck is he doing in an old lady's cottage? I quietly open the door to the cottage and peer inside. The wolf is fast asleep and his belly is large and bloated. I wonder who he has eaten this time.

Without even thinking, I just grab a pair of scissors off a table and carefully and quietly cut open the sleeping wolf's stomach. To my surprise, not one but *two* people are inside. Boy, do they love me!!! It seems like ages before they get finished thanking me and hugging me.

Finally, I get them to listen. I say, "We have to act fast and teach the wolf a lesson. I know just what to do. Let's gather stones quickly." We place the stones in the wolf's stomach, and then Grandma sews him up.

We run outside and hide. Then we hear a giant burp from the cottage and the wolf stumbles out. I'm so relieved to hear him moaning as he disappears into the forest. I don't think this guy is going to be eating any more humans any time soon. He looks miserable!

Fact vs. Opinion, page 13

1. fact	9. opinion	17. fact	25. fact
2. opinion	10. opinion	18. opinion	26. opinion
3. fact	11. fact	19. fact	
4. opinion	12. fact	20. fact	
5. opinion	13. opinion	21. fact	
6. opinion	14. opinion	22. fact	
7. opinion	15. opinion	23. opinion	
8. fact	16. opinion	24. opinion	

Propaganda Techniques, page 15-16

1. Plain folk
2. Transfer
3. Repetition
4. Bandwagon
5. Plain folk

Art and Persuasion, page 20

Answers will vary. Here is one possibility:

Guernica, by Pablo Picasso, is an anti-war painting. It shows the depravity of war with its images of twisted people and animals. The people and animals look as if they are screaming in pain. There is even an image of a mother screaming with what looks like a limp baby in her arms. There is a man trampled with a broken sword in his arm. Strangely, there is also a man coming through the door with a light. He maybe represents hope in the world. The images send a message of torture and horror. The black and white in the picture adds to the stark and cold look of the painting. Picasso is protesting war.

Declaring Yourself, page 23

Answers will vary. Here is one possibility:

1. **The Environment:** Both corporations and individuals should take measures to protect the environment.
2. **Music Sharing on the Internet:** Music sharing on the Internet is good for the music industry because it enhances creativity.
3. **Going on a diet:** Dieting makes people really cranky and isn't worth it.
4. **Censorship:** Censorship of any kind violates the First Amendment.
5. **Country music:** Country music speaks the truth about how most Americans really feel about the world.

Because I Said So, page 27-28

Answers will vary. Here is one possibility:

Argument: It's hard being the oldest brother or sister in a family.
1. It is hard because you usually get blamed for what goes wrong.
2. It is hard because you are expected to be a good, responsible role model for your younger sibling.
3. It is hard because you always have to help the littler ones and nobody ever helps you.

Argument: The state should lower the driving age to 14.
1. It should lower it because fourteen and fifteen year olds are very busy, and their parents get tired of driving them everywhere.
2. It should lower it because fourteen and fifteen year olds could be more helpful to their parents by being able to run errands.
3. It should lower it because fourteen and fifteen year olds are much more mature than teenagers used to be.

Argument: Being a vegetarian is not a wise choice for teenagers.
1. It is not a wise choice because teenagers are still growing and need lots of protein.
2. It is not a wise choice because parents generally refuse to cook their teenage children special vegetarian meals.
3. It is not a wise choice because it is hard to be a teenager without eating pepperoni pizza and cheeseburgers.

Argument: P.E. class is an important part of school.
1. It is important because nutrition experts recommend that people get exercise every day.
2. It is important because students need a physical break from all of the thinking they have to do in school.
3. It is important because P.E. helps promote a good habit of physical fitness.

Follow-up

Argument: Schools should have no tolerance for guns at school.

1. Schools should have no tolerance for guns at school because school should be a safe place, and guns can be dangerous.
2. Schools should have no tolerance for guns at school because there is no appropriate reason to have one at school, even during hunting season.
3. Schools should have no tolerance for guns at school because accidents can occur.

Argument: We must start now to do more to protect our environment.

1. We must start now to do more to protect our environment because our air, water and soil are getting rapidly worse.
2. We must start now to do more to protect our environment because our current environmental conditions are harming people's health.
3. We must start now to do more to protect our environment because we are destroying animal species and forever changing our ecosystems.

Argument: Popular music is a thing of the past.

1. Popular music is a thing of the past because there is so much music available now that is much better than what is considered popular.
2. Popular music is a thing of the past because the Internet makes it possible to listen to a wide variety of music outside of the Top 40.
3. Popular music is a thing of the past because people want the freedom to choose their own music, rather than listen to only what is dictated by the music industry.

Taking Notes, page 50-51

Answers will vary. Here is one possibility:

1. A summary: Wal-Mart has a negative impact on communities that allow it to establish itself in their towns. Wal-Mart increases productivity and offers some of the lowest prices, compared to other retailers, in the country.
2. "...some economists credit Wal-Mart's low prices with suppressing inflation"
3. Productivity rates have gone up throughout our economy, and this is because of Wal-Mart, according to experts.

Plagiarism Quiz, page 56

1. **TRUE.** Whenever you take information, ideas or exact quotes from a source, you must give credit for the information.
2. **FALSE.** You are committing plagiarism any time you copy information without giving credit.
3. **FALSE.** Rewriting something in your own handwriting doesn't make it your work.
4. **TRUE.** When you take an idea from another source, you must give that source credit, whether or not you are using the exact words. (The only exception to this is information that is common knowledge.)
5. **TRUE.** Plagiarism is generally considered a misdemeanor. There are situations where those found guilty can be fined and spend time in jail.
6. **TRUE.** Those convicted of plagiarism can be fined anywhere from $100 to $50,000.
7. **TRUE.** Schools have different policies on plagiarism, including punishments as harsh as expulsion.
8. **FALSE.** It is plagiarism any time you try to pass off someone else's work as your own.
9. **FALSE.** It may be an honest mistake to forget to put quotation marks around words someone else said or wrote, but it is also plagiarism.
10. **FALSE.** Changing one or two words is not enough to avoid plagiarizing. Even if you completely rewrite everything a person said but are still using that writer's idea, you must still give the original author credit.
11. **TRUE.** You should always place quotation marks around exact quotations and give the source of the quotation.

12. **TRUE.** It is always important to understand your research enough to write it into your own words. However, you should still cite where you found the original information.

13. **FALSE.** Even if your plagiarism is accidental, it is still plagiarism.

14. **FALSE.** All original works, with or without a copyright symbol (©), are protected under copyright laws.

15. **TRUE.** There are many new web sites and software programs that help teachers detect plagiarism. However, many teachers are very good at detecting plagiarism, even without using technology.

Think Elbows, pages 61-62

Answers will vary. Here is one possibility:

1. The room I share with my sister is wallpapered with Nelly posters, yet I can't stand Nelly. Therefore, the posters should come down.

2. While many adults argue that teenagers watch too much television, most teenagers have responsibilities like work, homework, sports practice, music lessons or play practice. Clearly, teenagers don't have time to watch too much television.

3. Since I am a hard worker and good student, responsible and enthusiastic, and a not-so-nerdy bookworm, the Thurgood Marshall Public Library should hire me for the summer.

4. Phoenix Suns' Shaquille O'Neal is over 7 feet tall. Although he is one of the biggest players in the NBA and one of the top ranked players in the sport, he can't make his free throws.

5. I think that eggs, waffles and Pop Tarts are gross. Furthermore, bacon, cinnamon toast and grapefruit halves are disgusting. Since I can't find any breakfast food I would want to choke down, I usually prefer to skip breakfast.

Synthesizing Information, page 64

Answers will vary. Here is one possibility:

Poverty rates are on the rise. According to information compiled by America's Second Harvest, poverty rose from 11.3 to 11.7% of the population between 2000 and 2001. It also reports that food banks across the country have had an 86% increase in requests for food assistance over the past year. In addition, the USDA reports that the number of "food insecure" American households rose from 14.8 to 16.1% in 2001. A "food insecure" household is a household that does not always have enough food for an active, healthy life.

Ethos, Pathos and Logos, page 66

Answers will vary. Here is one possibility:

Ethos: Dr. Berry, my physics teacher, always says, "Crystal is such a good kid. I wish there were more like her."
Pathos: Pancho and I were the best of friends, especially since I don't have too many people friends.
Logos: I walked Pancho every day and will do the same with any new kitty.

Dear Small and Sometimes Furry Pet Shop:

I was in your store ten days ago and purchased a sweet box turtle that I named Marigold. Your friendly staff helped me pick out all the equipment, supplies and food I would need to provide Marigold with a safe and happy home. I grew very attached to Marigold because she never judged me and always listened to my stories, unlike my brothers and sisters who yell at me to leave them alone or else. So it was a very sad day when, to my horror, I discovered Marigold dead.

My parents have trusted me to take care of our dog, Henry, for a number of years now. Mom and Dad know they can count on me to feed, walk and love Henry without reminding me a million times a day. I often animal sit for our neighbors Sally and John Quincy. Mrs. Quincy even said to my parents, "Shannon has proved herself to be a true animal lover. We trust her implicitly with the care of our animals."

I fed Marigold according to the schedule your store manager gave me. Clean, fresh water was always available, her aquarium was kept clean and she also had a heat lamp. As you can see I am a responsible pet owner. I did not neglect or mistreat Marigold and would appreciate a refund for her premature death.

Sincerely,

Shannon Shell

The Rebuttal, page 69

Answers will vary. Here is one possibility:

2. Although some people are crazy about a Starbucks Mochachinos, I prefer to stick with skinny lattes.
3. While a vegetarian diet is probably better for you, I could never give up triple threat meatball sandwiches.
4. Mom says it would look tacky to get my nose pierced, yet I think it looks elegant.
5. Everyone I know wants a big monster SUV, but my dream car is a little purple Saturn.

I Feel Wishy-Washy, page 70

Dear gooeylouie@hotmail.com:

Eddie, you are the one for me and I am the one for you. You are always looking at me in Mrs. Dietz's class. We are a match made in heaven. Even though you are always in in-school suspension, you are a good person deep down inside. My mom and my best friend Shelby don't agree, but they don't know you like I do. We should declare our love to the whole school by going to the Fall Festival together. What do you think?

Love,

Diamondprincess4567@yahoo.com (Clarissa)

Follow-up

Dear Clarissa:

You need to stop chasing after Eddie because he is nothing but trouble. He is always in in-school suspension because he doesn't have any respect for teachers. He is constantly late for class, he talks on his cell phone during school hours, and he has been caught cheating on tests more than once. Is this somebody you want to be associated with?

Also, Eddie is not always looking at you in Mrs. Dietz's class. I know this because I've watched him for the past week. What he is actually doing is looking past you to watch Andy Weggerman hurl spit wads at the ceiling.

Your mom is very concerned about your fascination with Eddie, too. She told me you are always talking about him at home, and she is worried that you are going to get into the same kind of trouble as Eddie. Do not go to the Fall Festival with Eddie because you will only regret it later. Please come with Sasha and me and you'll have a much better time. Plus, Eddie is grounded for a month and won't be able to go anyway!

Your friend,

Shelby

Kind of . . . Sort of, page 71

Answers will vary. Here is one possibility:

Principal Gomez, teachers, students and honored guests:

I want to talk to you about my qualifications for student council president. I would be the best person for the job because I love this school. Don't you agree that a student council president should feel strongly about her school? I feel that I'm qualified because I am a good student and I've served on the student council for the past two years. So, if you love this school, vote for me for student council president. Thank you.

Follow-up

Principal Gomez, teachers, students and honored guests:

I am running for student council president because I am the best qualified for the position. I think this school is the best in the county and I am willing to work to keep it there. I am a good student, I play point guard on the basketball team, and I've served on the student council for the two years I've been here. I am a volunteer on several committees for students and faculty members. I am also a good listener. If you want to bring important issues to the administration, I am the person who will listen to you and make sure we students are properly represented. So remember me when it comes time to vote and vote yes for me on voting day.

Thank you. You won't regret it!

About the Author

Dawn DiPrince loves to teach writing. She has helped many people—from age 7 to 87—to become writers. She has taught poetry, journalism and other writing to middle school students at a local after-school program. And, through her autobiography writing classes, she has enjoyed teaching hundreds of adults to write their life stories. The former owner and editor of *BlueSky Quarterly* (a magazine that celebrates life in southeastern Colorado), DiPrince is now the Associate Director of the Sangre de Cristo Arts Center in Pueblo, Colorado. She loves her job because nearly 70 percent of her work day is spent writing.

DiPrince lives in Pueblo with her husband Chris Markuson; their two curious children, Max and Sophie; and their funny and sweet new baby Mario. They live one block away from her parents—both retired teachers.

More Great Books *from* Cottonwood Press

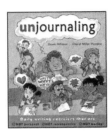 **UNJOURNALING**—Daily Writing Exercises that Are NOT Personal, NOT Introspective, NOT Boring! The more than 200 impersonal but engaging writing prompts in this exercise book help students practice their writing skills without asking them to share personal thoughts they would rather keep to themselves.

 **HOW TO HANDLE DIFFICULT PARENTS**—A teacher's survival guide. Suzanne Capek Tingley identifies characteristics of some parent "types". She then goes on to give practical, easy-to-implement methods of working with them more effectively.

 **A SENTENCE A DAY**—Short, playful proofreading exercises to help students avoid tripping up when they write. This book focuses on short, playful, interesting sentences with a sense of humor.

 **PHUNNY STUPH**—Your students will smile and sharpen their proofreading skills as they correct the jokes and urban legends. The activities contain just about every error you can imagine, from spelling and punctuation mistakes to sentence fragments and run-ons.

 **DOWN*WRITE* FUNNY**—Using student's love of the ridiculous to build serious writing skills. The entertaining activities and illustrations in this book help teach all kinds of useful writing skills.

 **RELUCTANT DISCIPLINARIAN**—Advice on classroom management from a softy who became (eventually) a successful teacher. Author Gary Rubinstein offers clear and specific advice for classroom management.

 **HOT FUDGE MONDAY**—Tasty Ways to Teach Parts of Speech to Students Who Have a Hard Time Swallowing Anything To Do With Grammar. This new edition includes quirky quizzes, extended writing activities, and Internet enrichment activities that reinforce new skills.

 **THINKING IN THREES**—The Power of Three in Writing. Faced with a writing task of any kind? Think of three things to say about the topic. Writing an essay? Remember that the body should have at least three paragraphs. Need help getting started? Learn three ways to begin an essay.

COTTONWOODPRESS INC.
www.cottonwoodpress.com